Face to Face

François and Jean Robert

Lars Müller Publishers

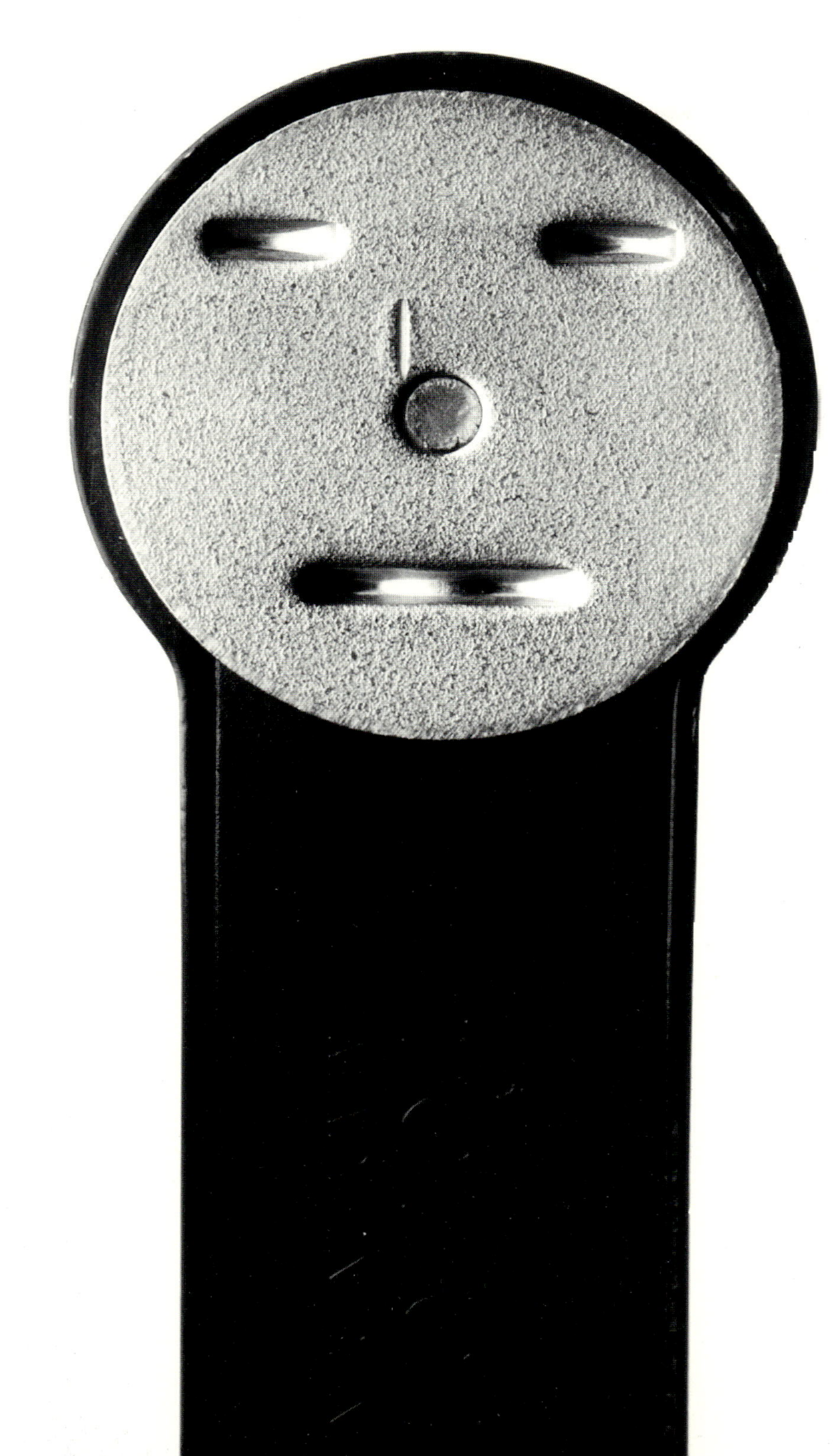

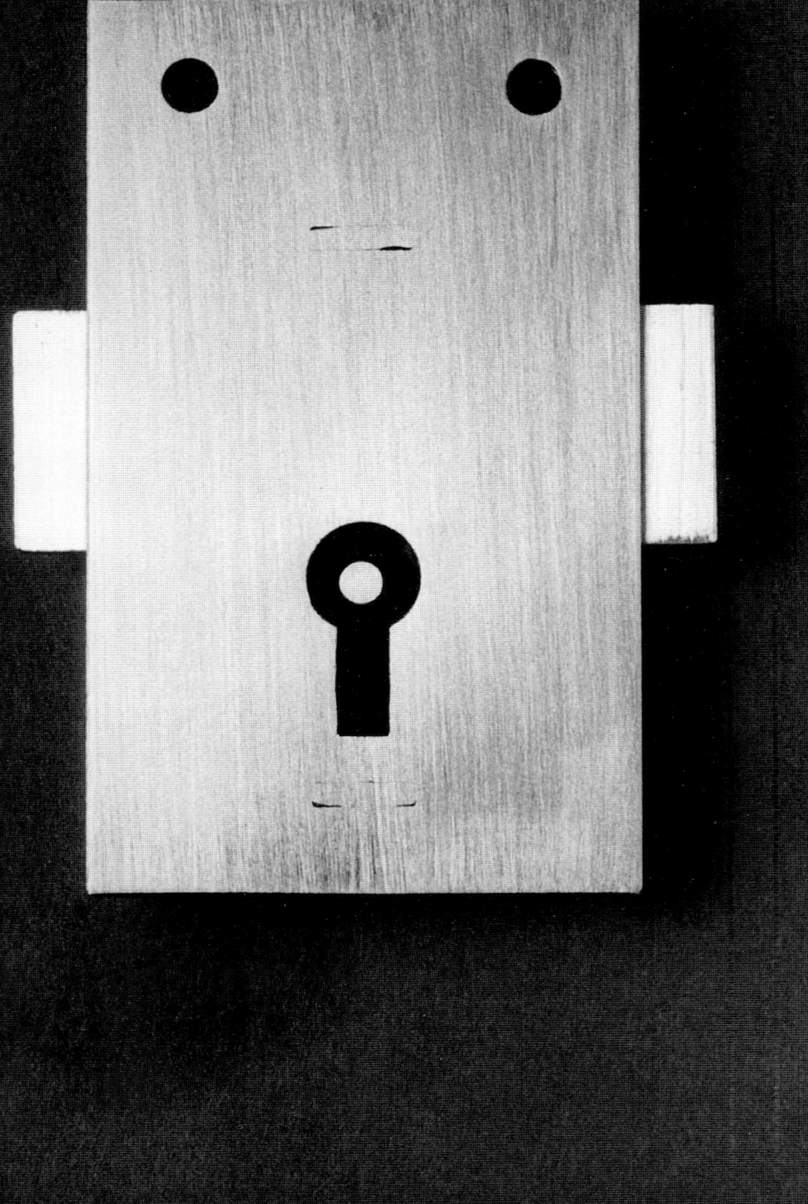

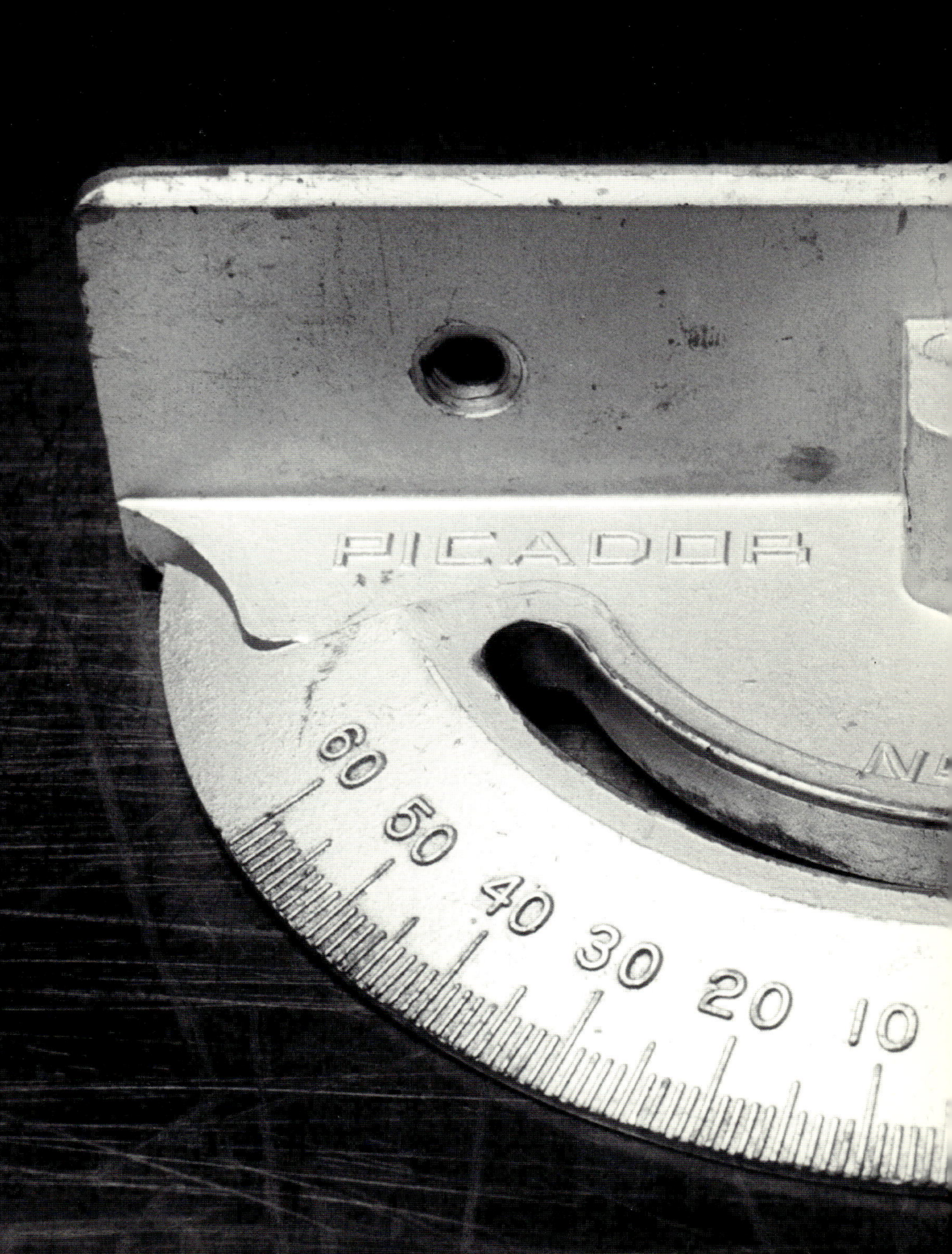
PICADOR
60
50
40
30
20
10

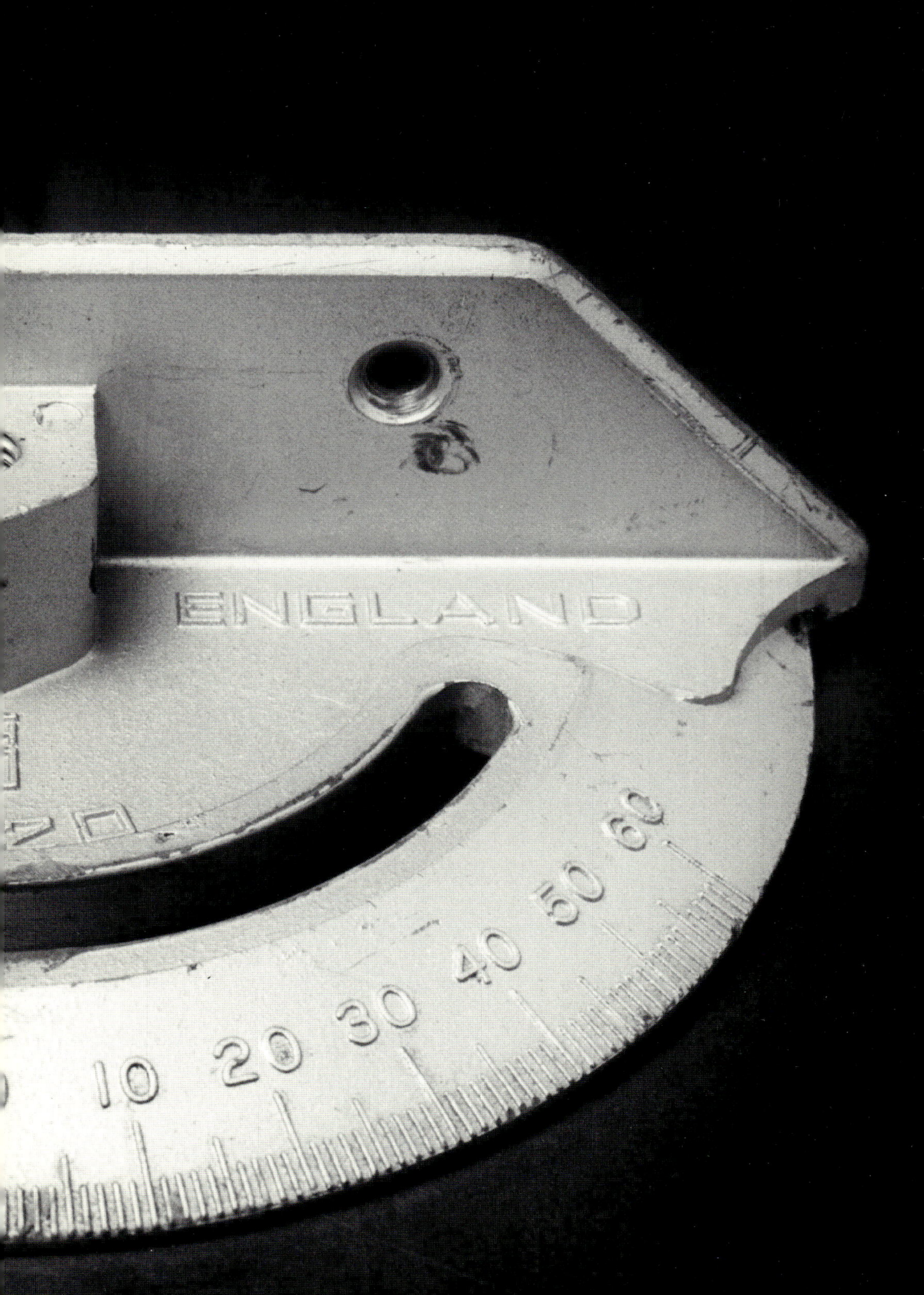
ENGLAND
10 20 30 40 50 60

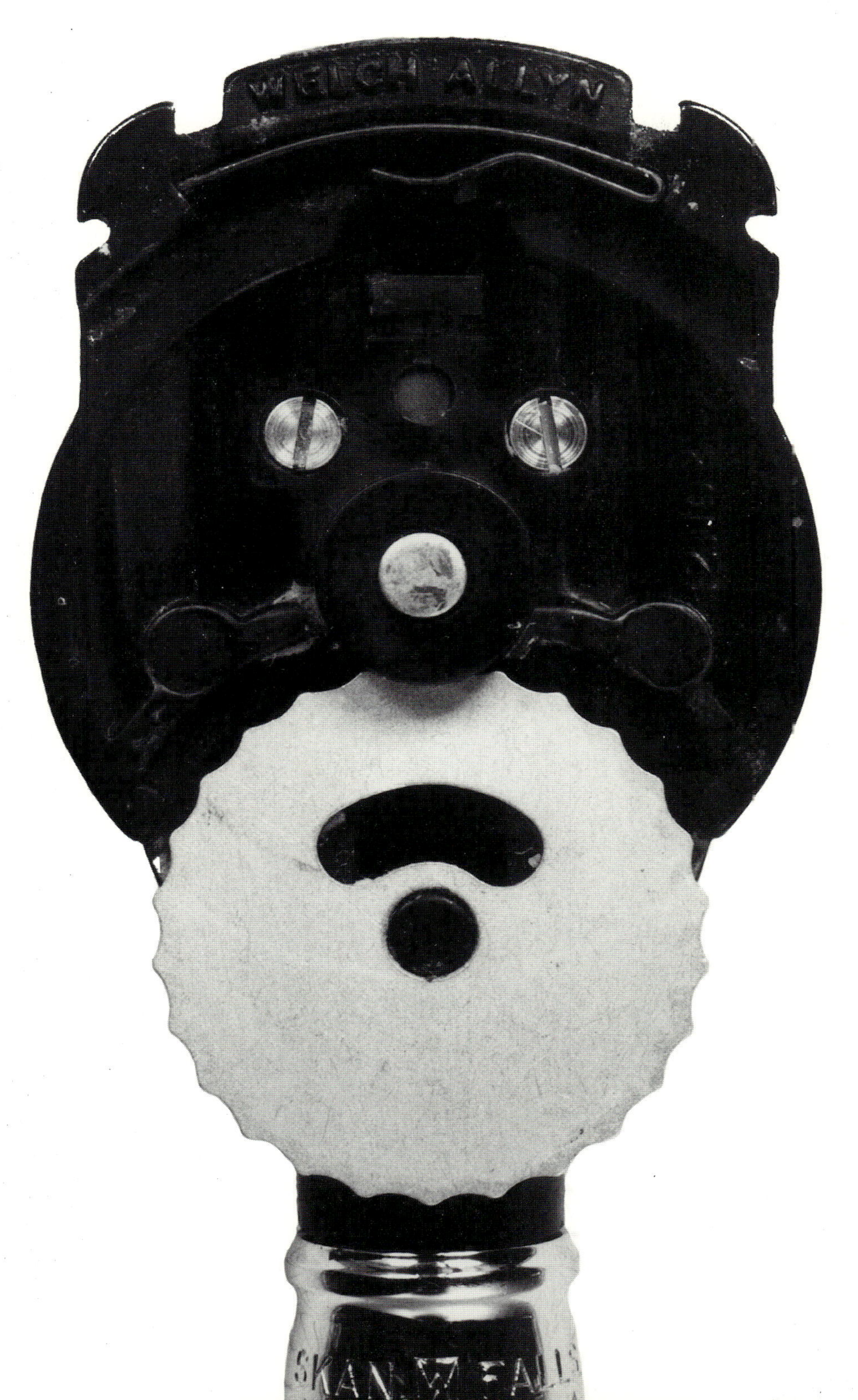
WELCH ALLYN
SKAN FALLS

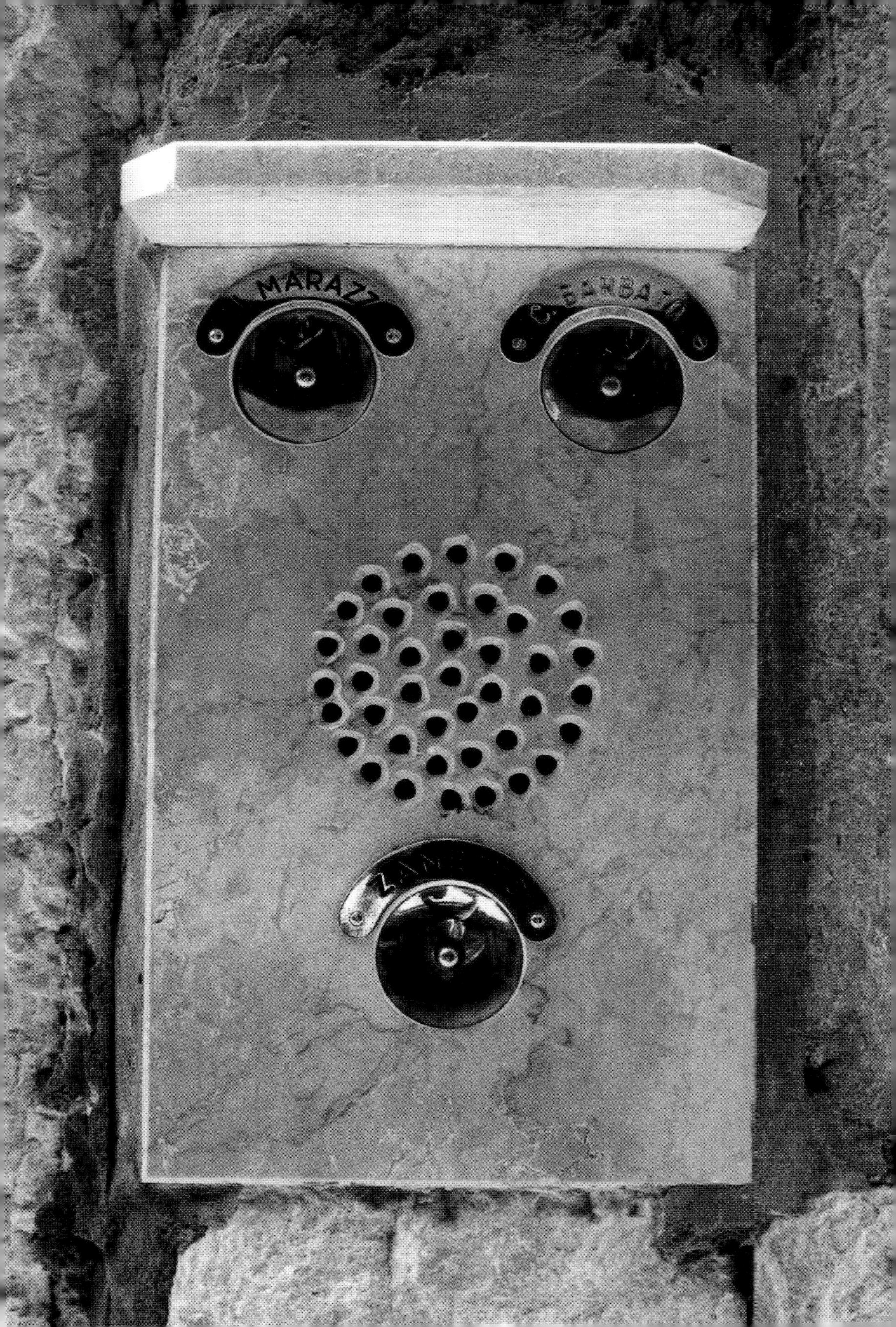

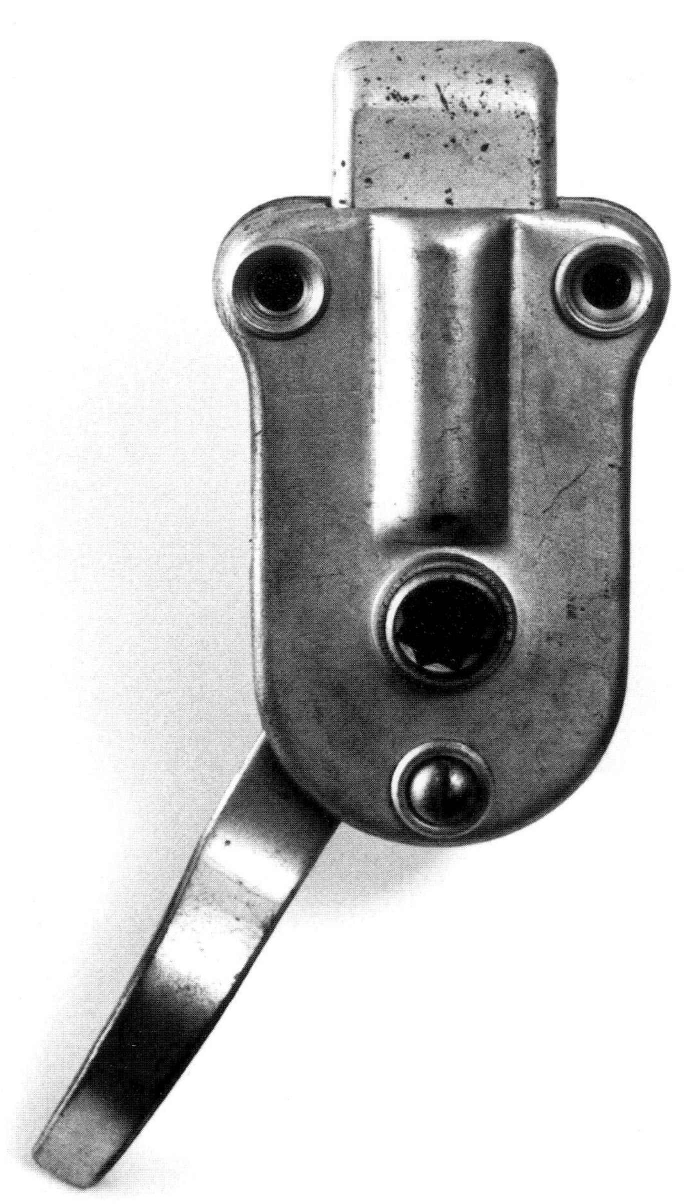

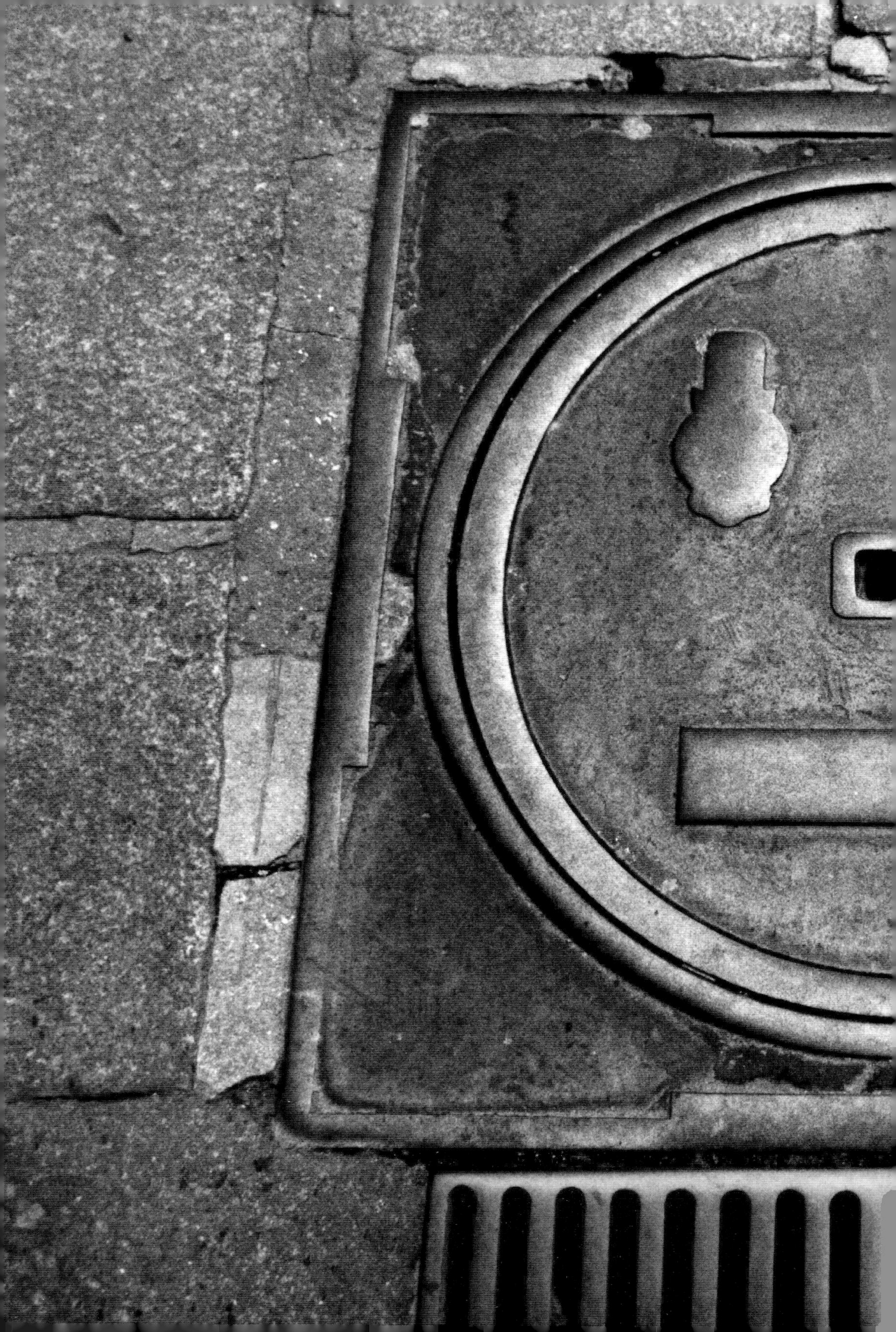

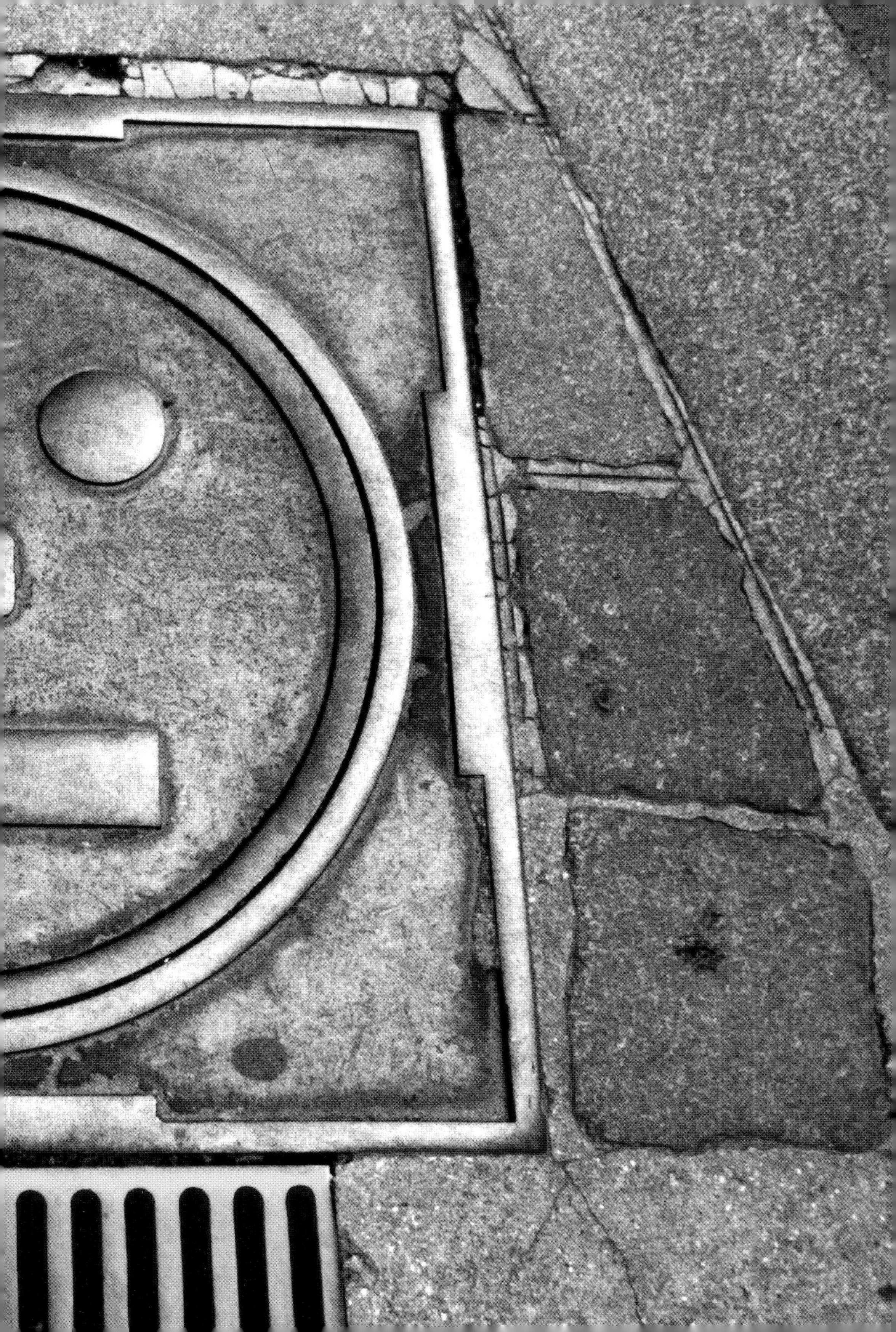

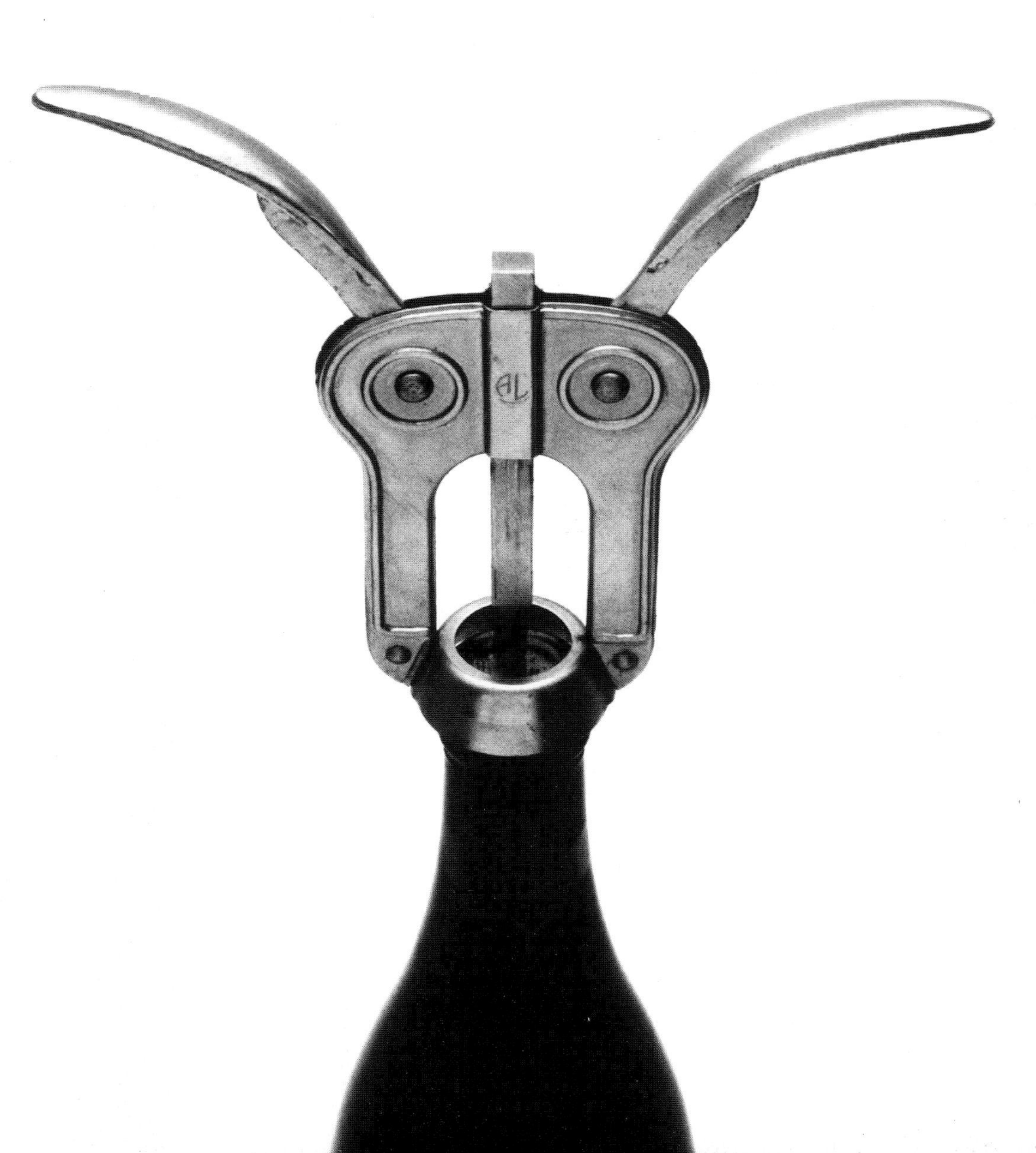

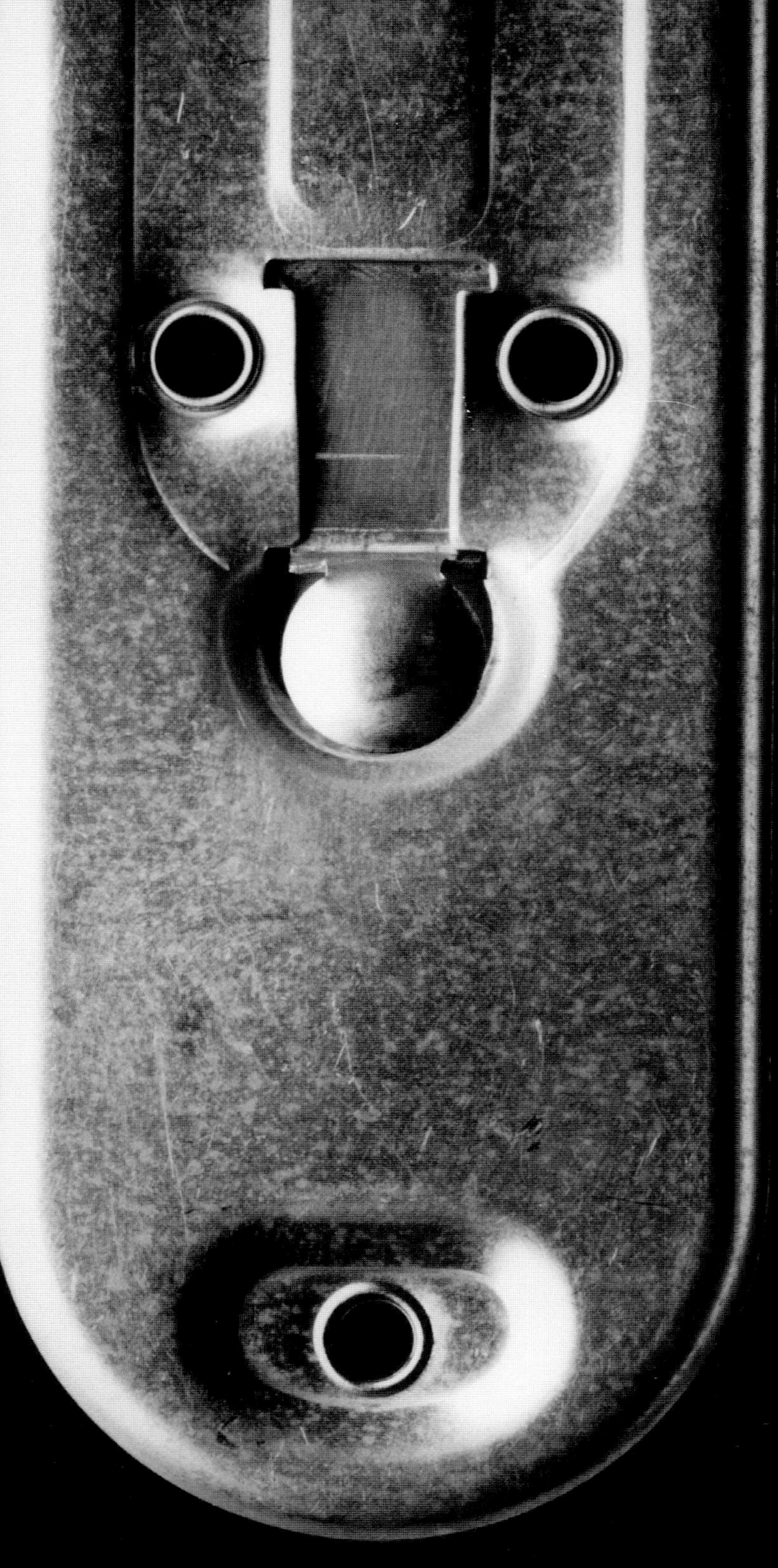

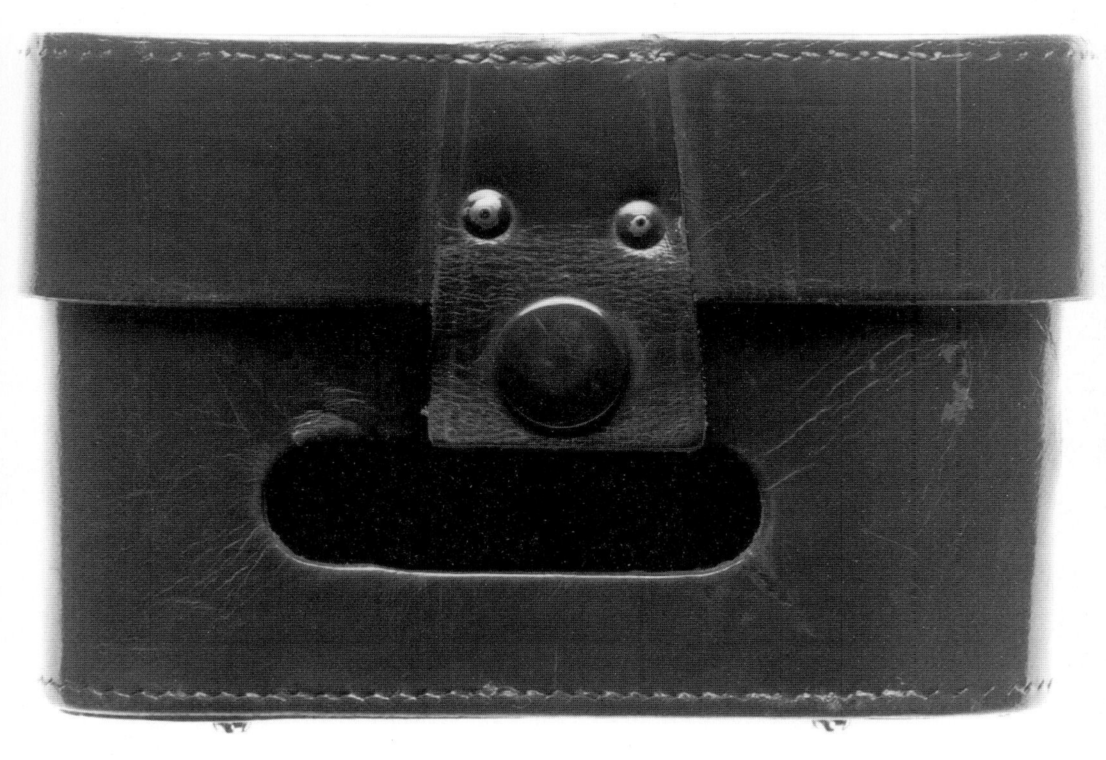

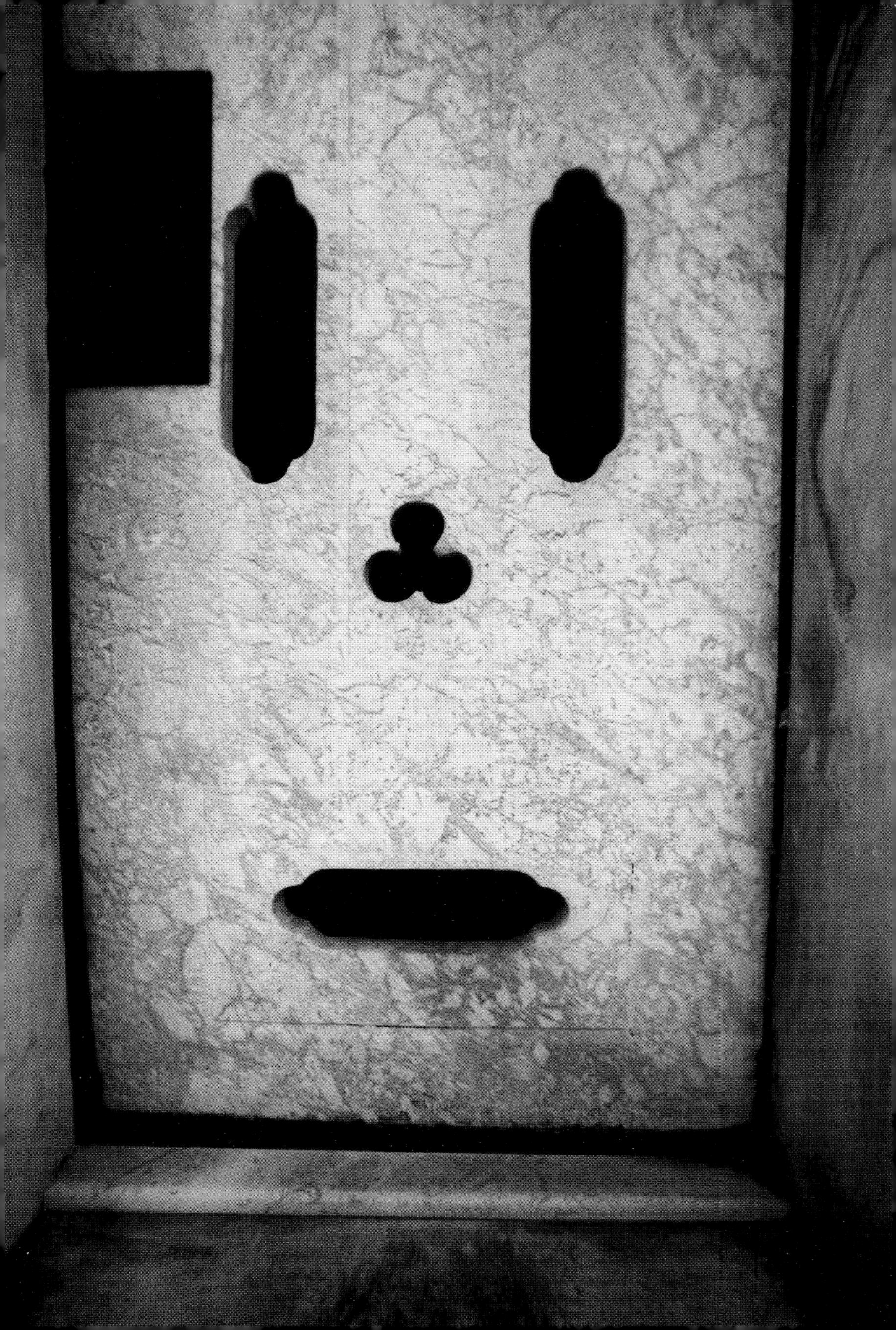

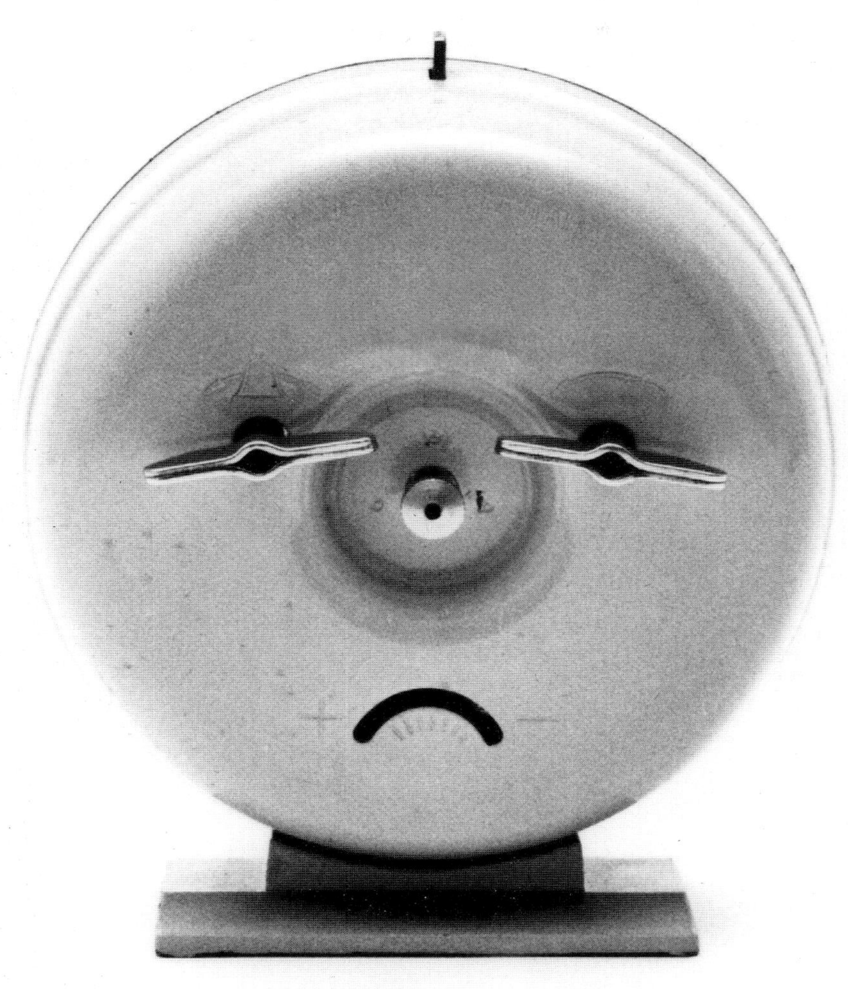

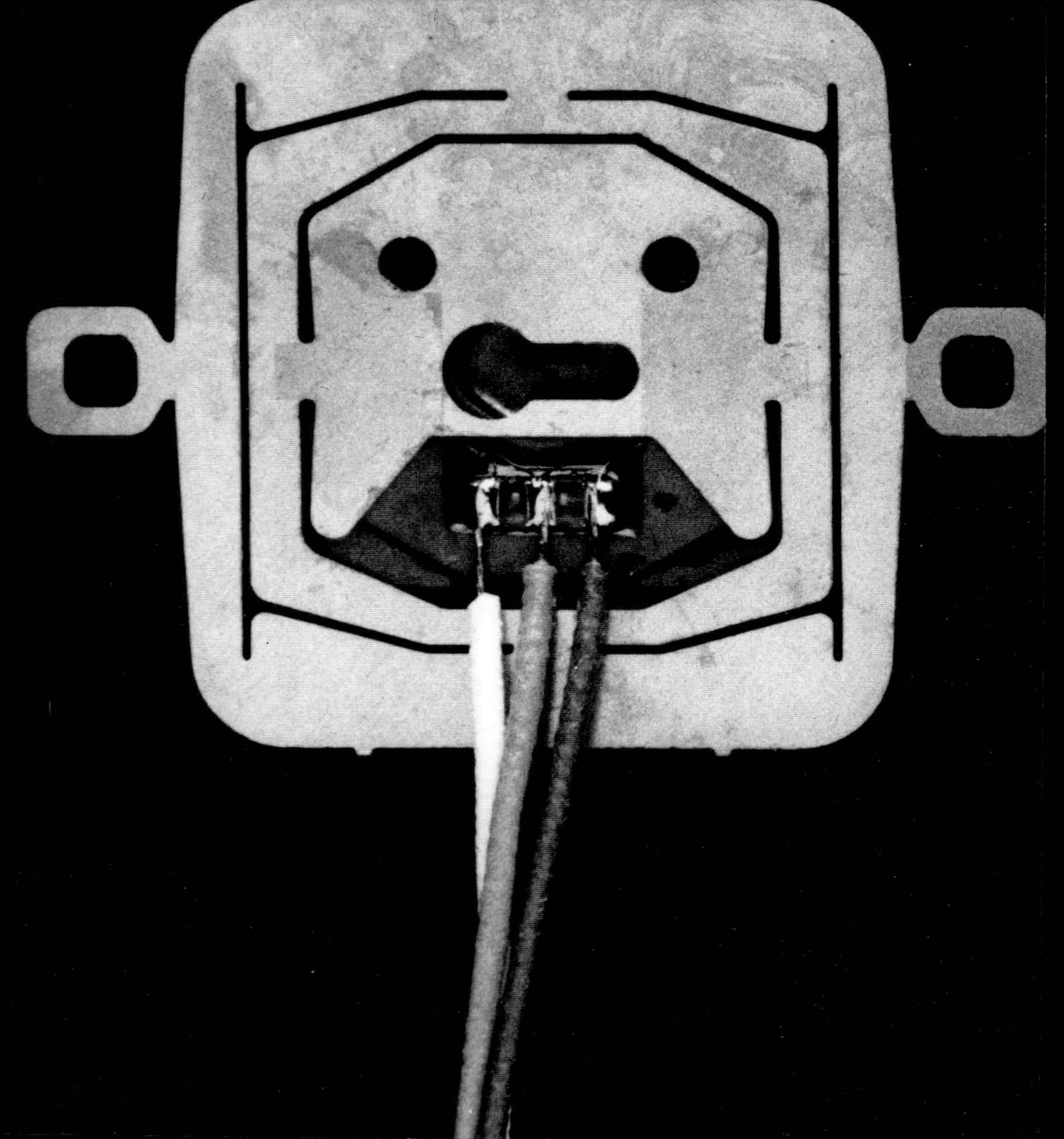

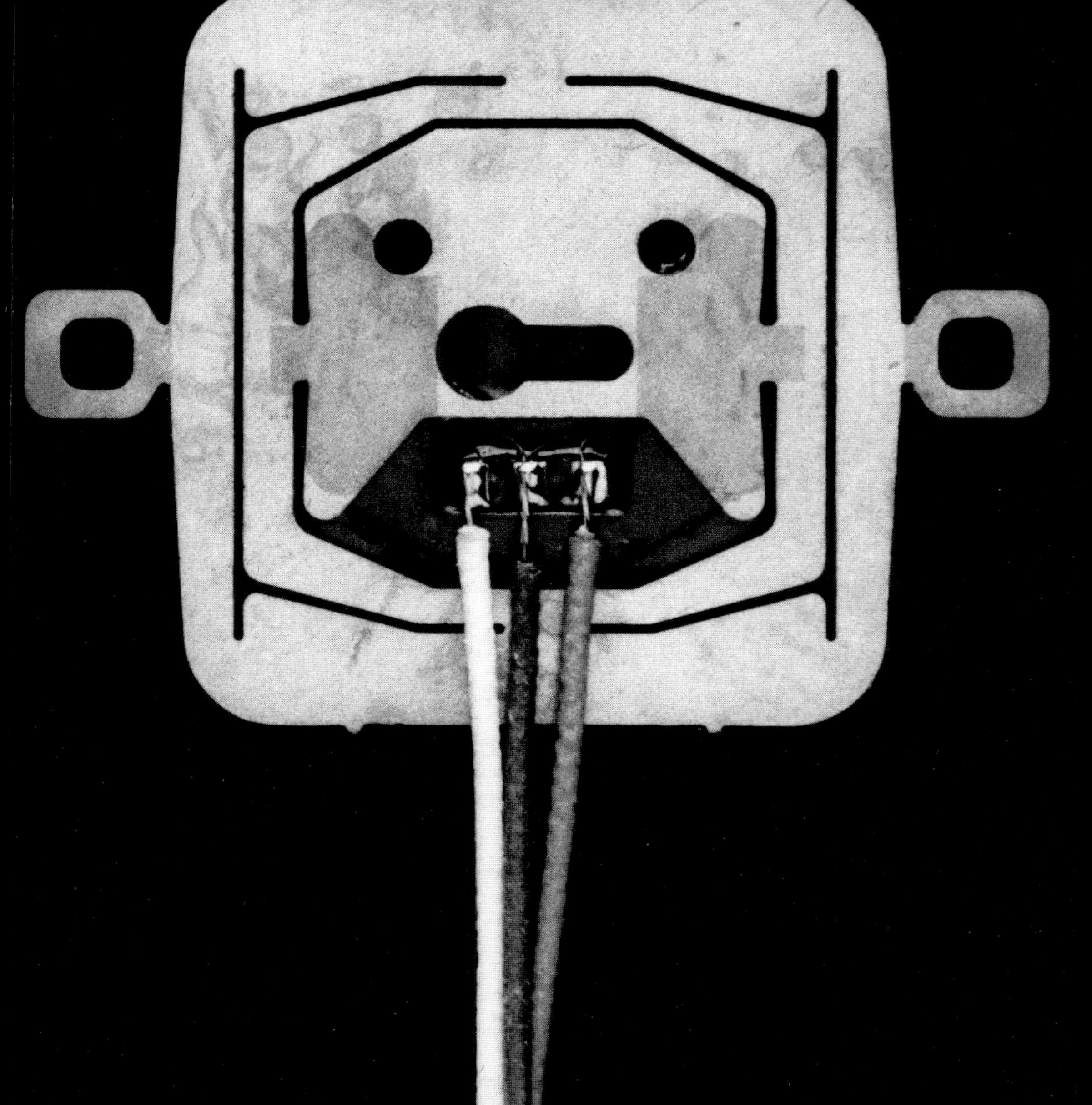

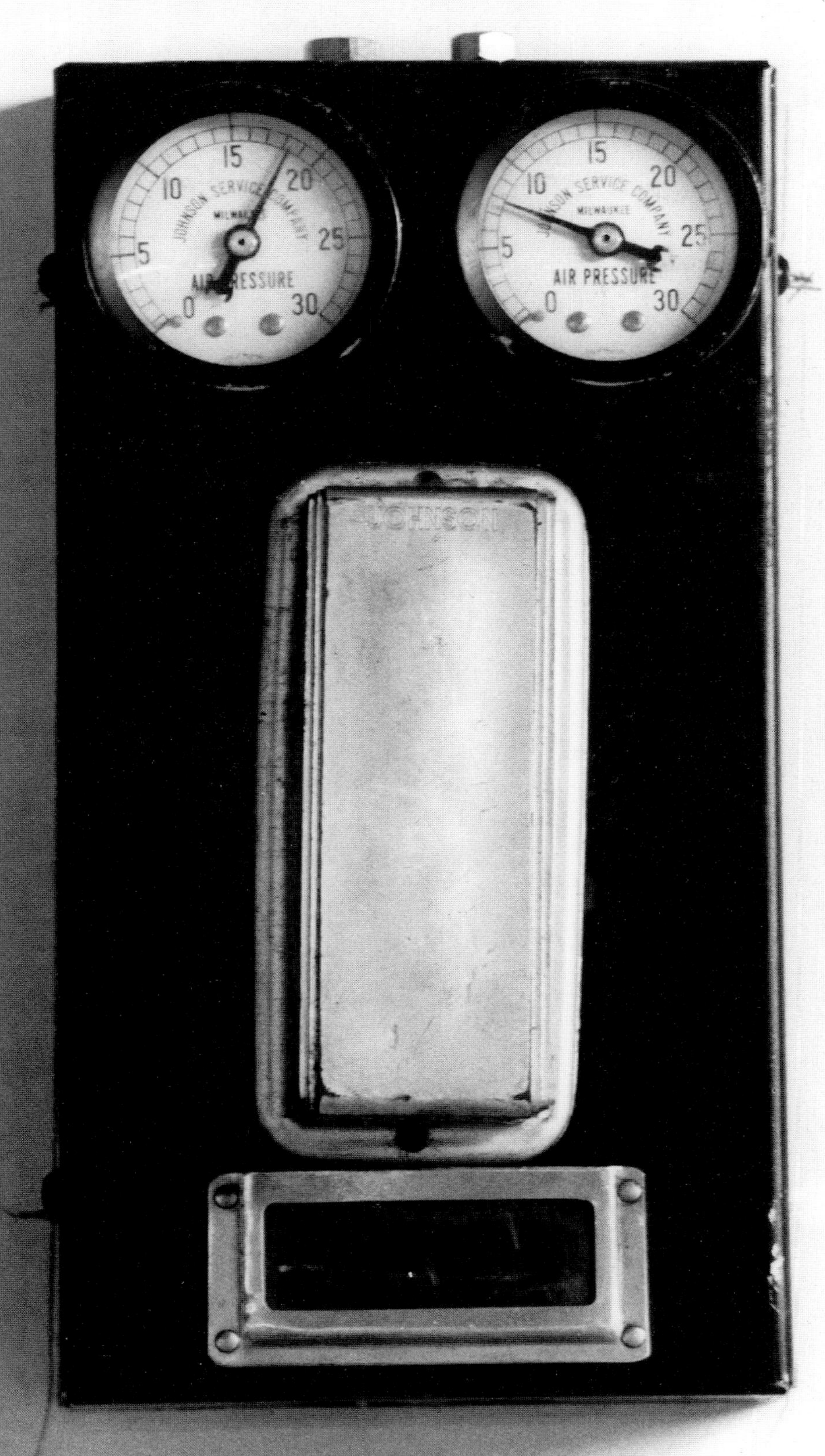

JOHNSON SERVICE COMPANY
MILWAUKEE
AIR PRESSURE
0 5 10 15 20 25 30
JOHNSON SERVICE COMPANY
MILWAUKEE
AIR PRESSURE
0 5 10 15 20 25 30
JOHNSON

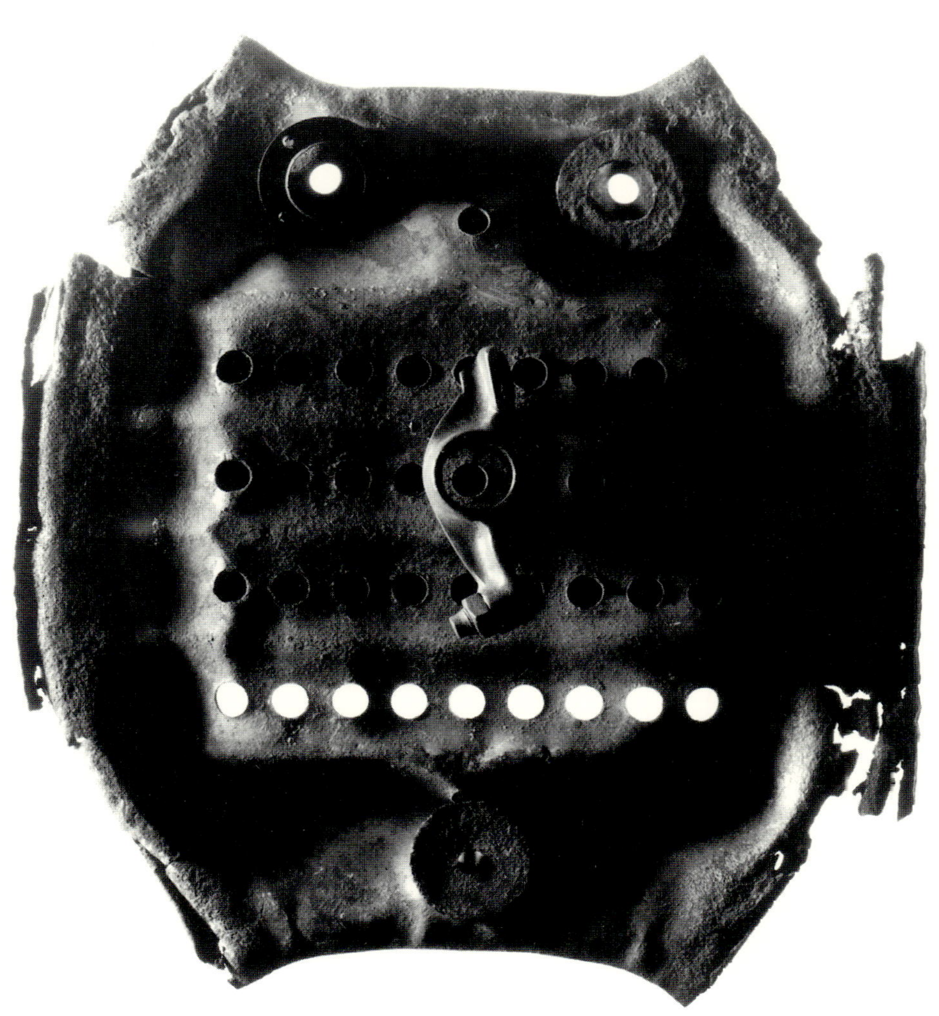

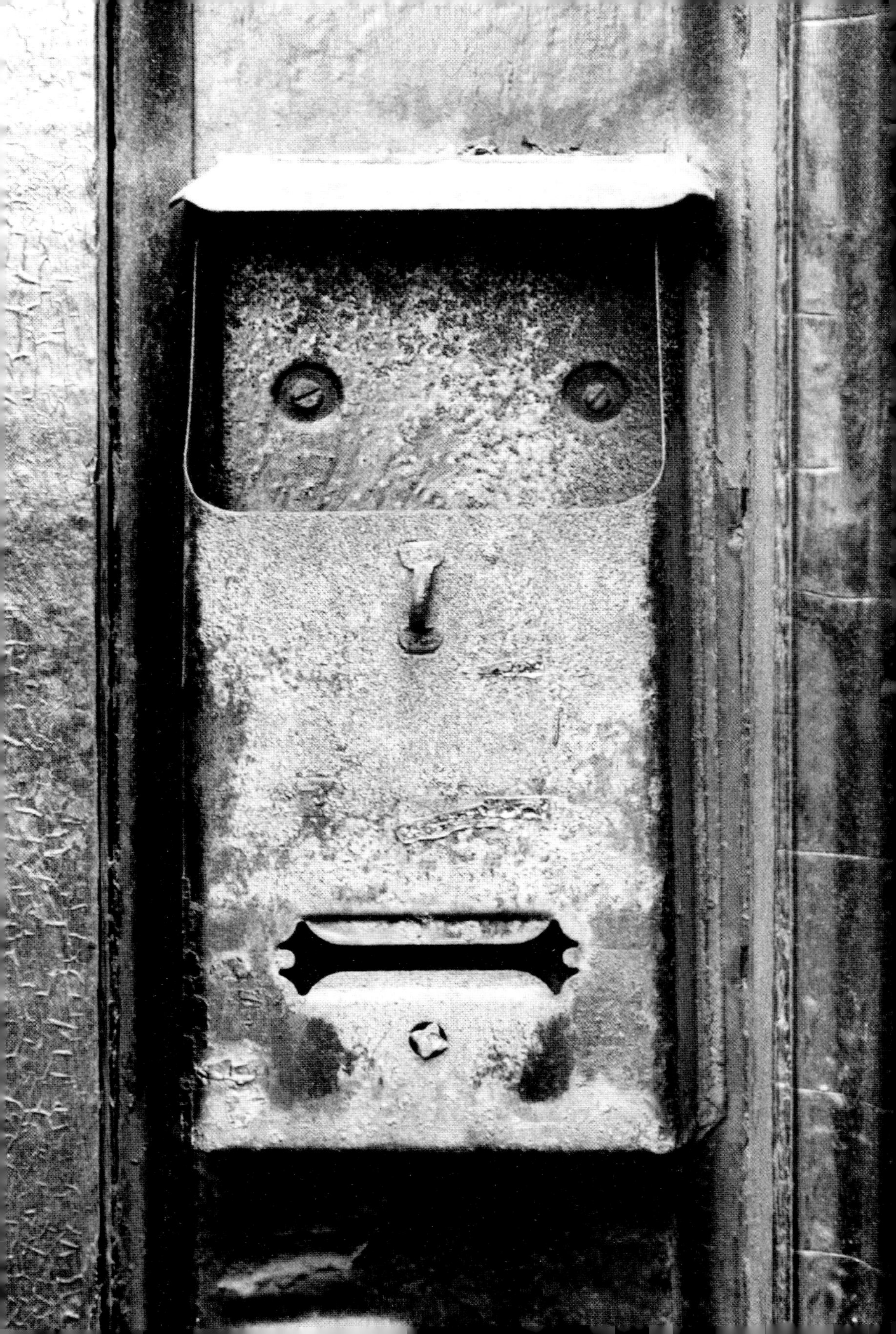

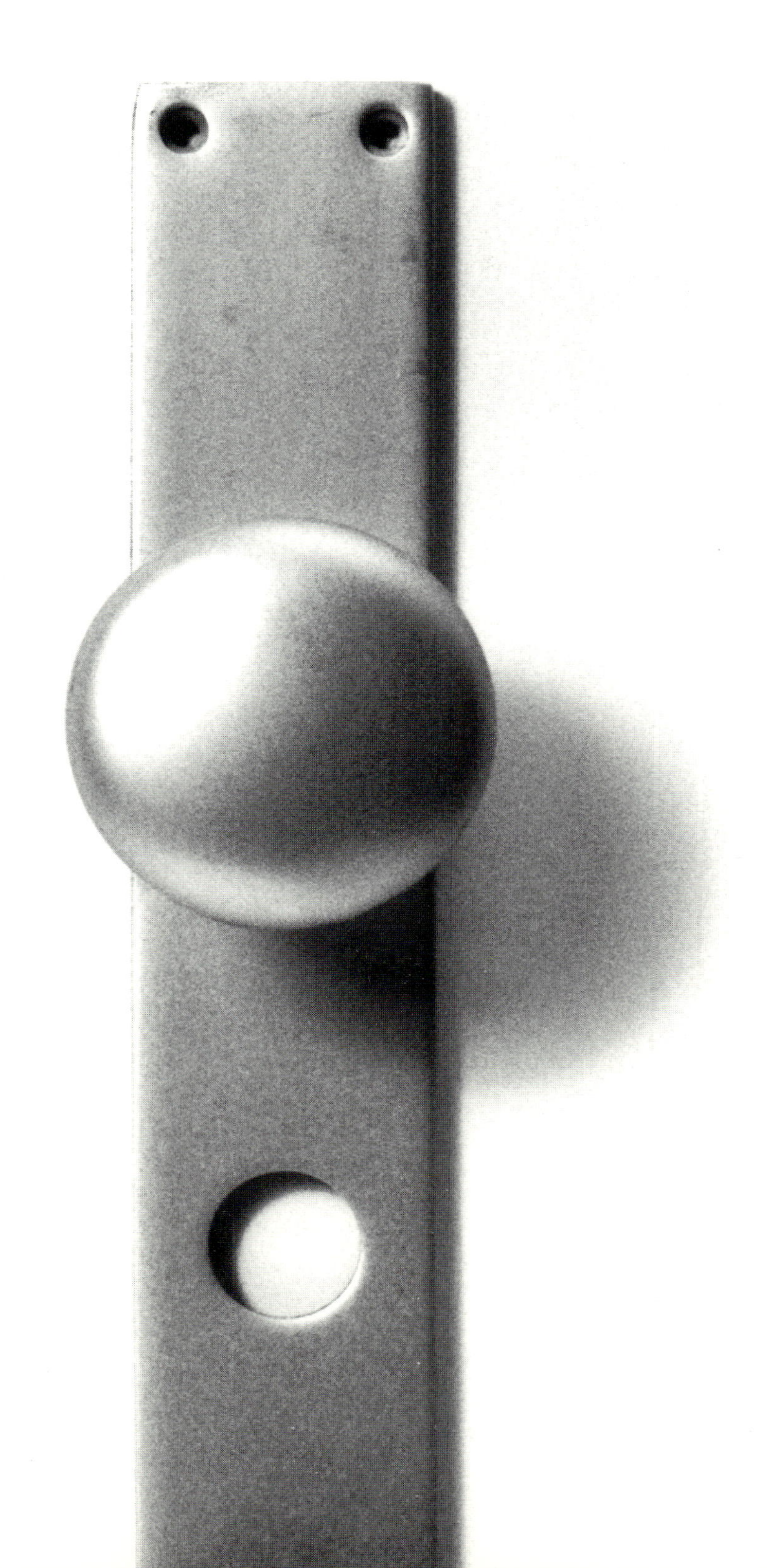

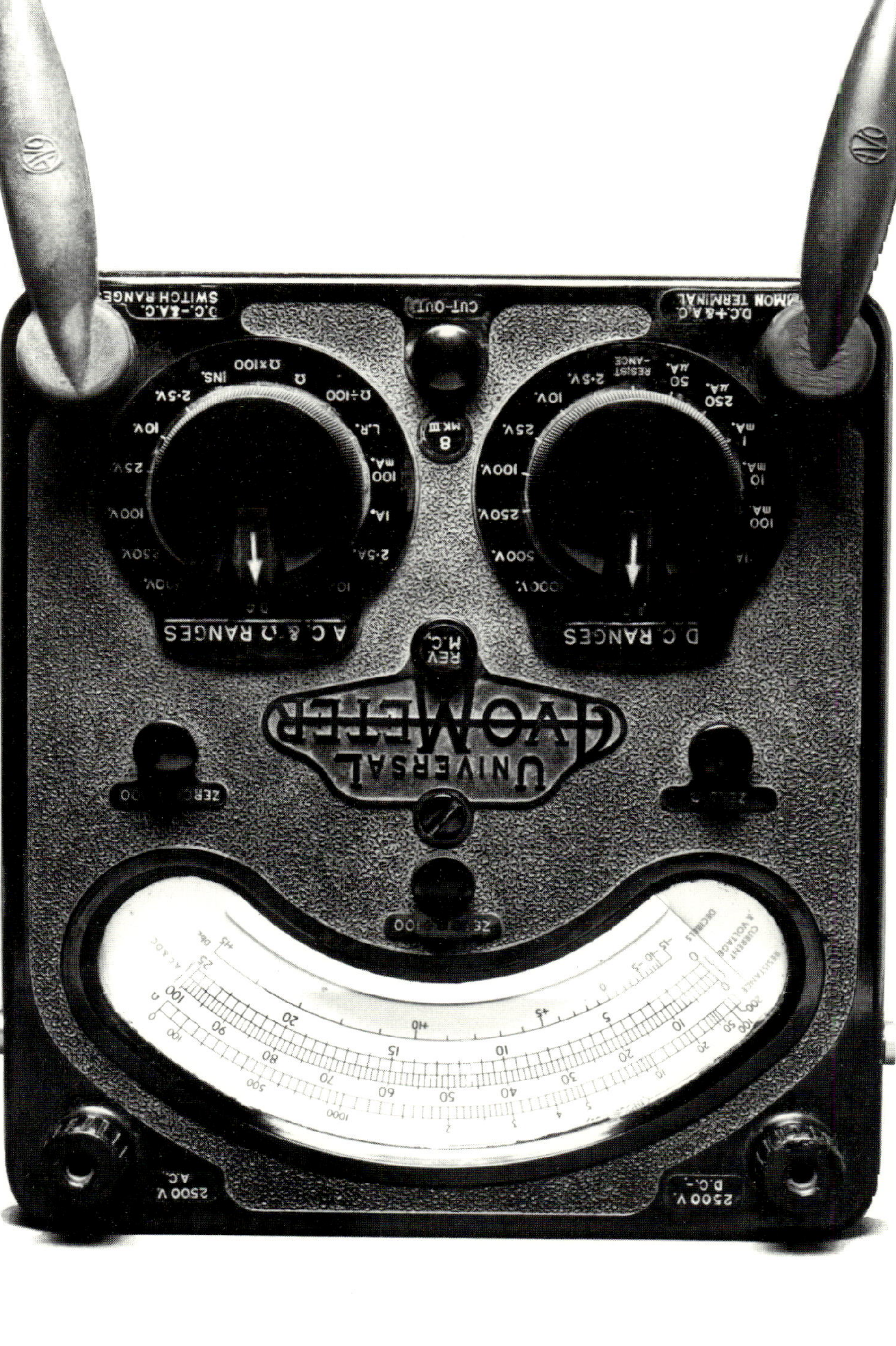

UNIVERSAL AVOMETER
A.C. & Ω RANGES
D.C. RANGES
CUT-OUT
REV M.C.
2500 V. A.C.
2500 V. D.C.

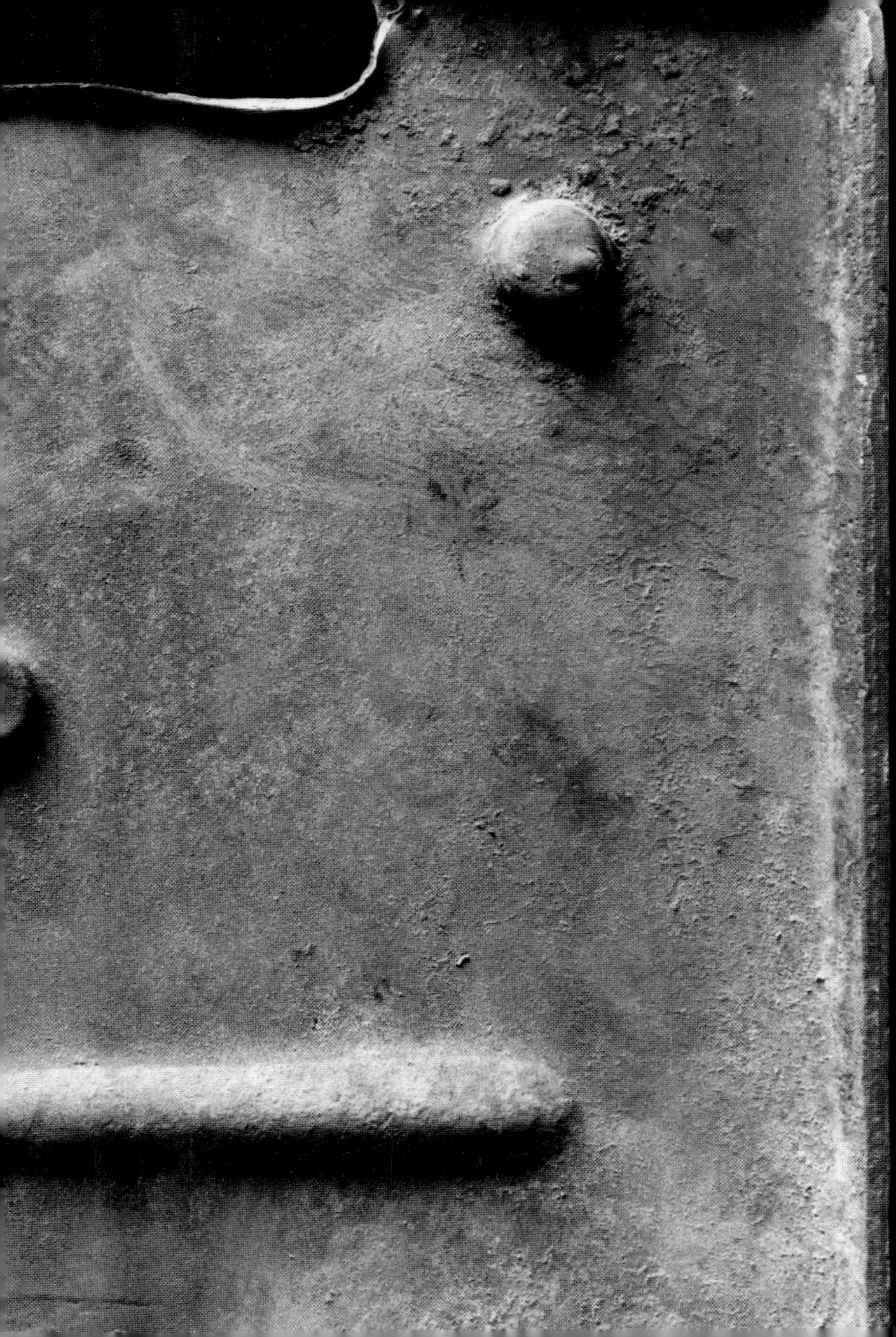

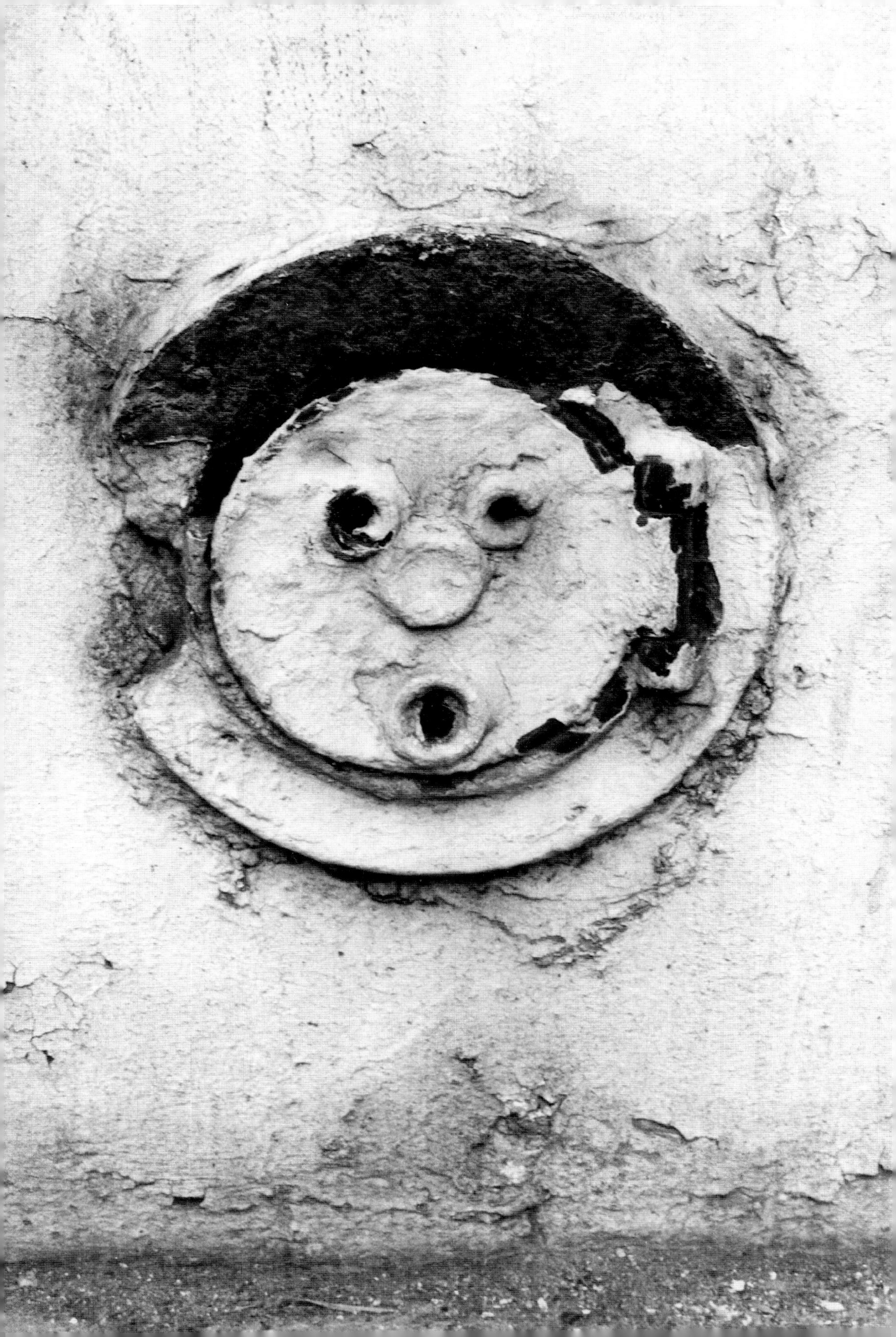

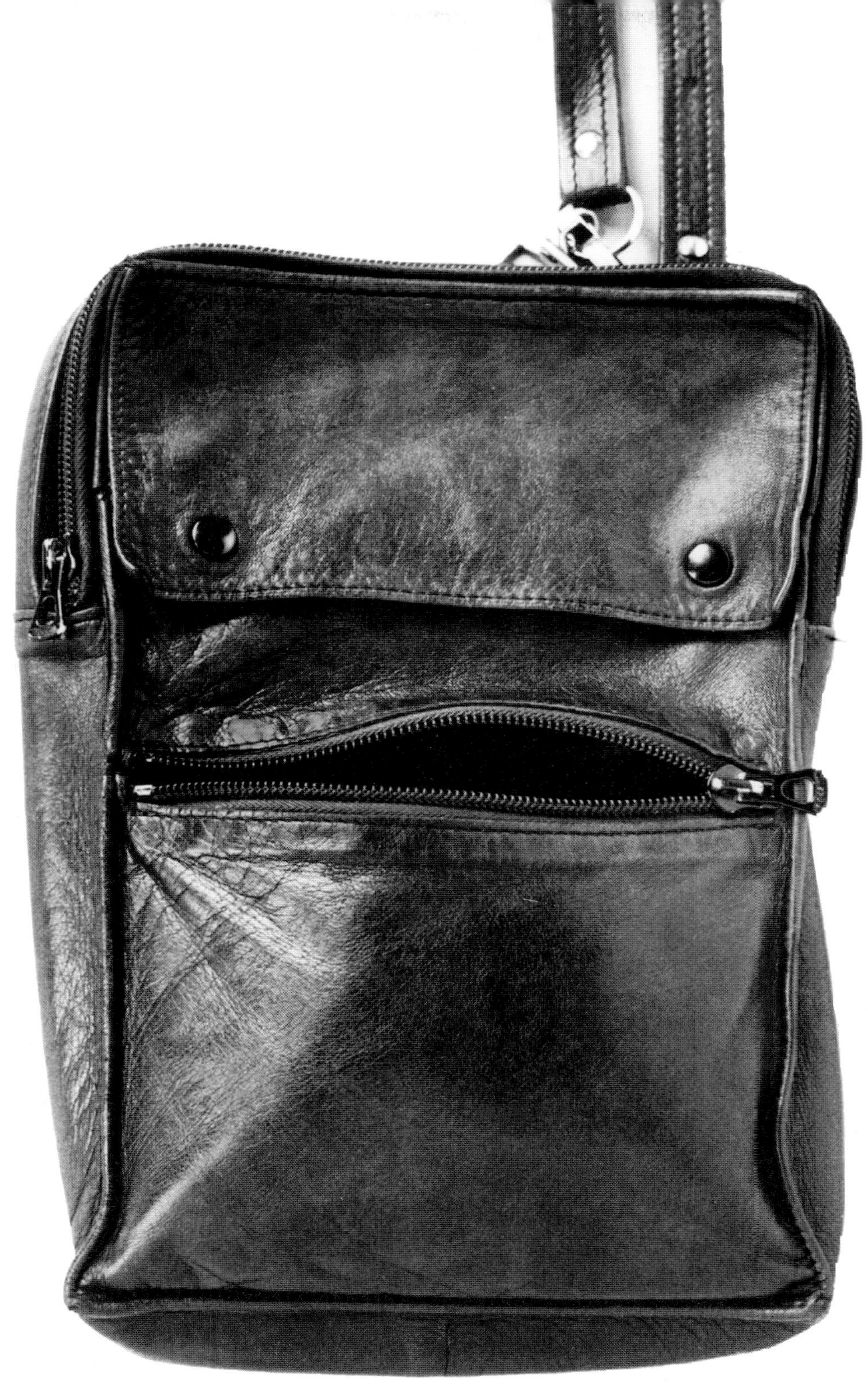

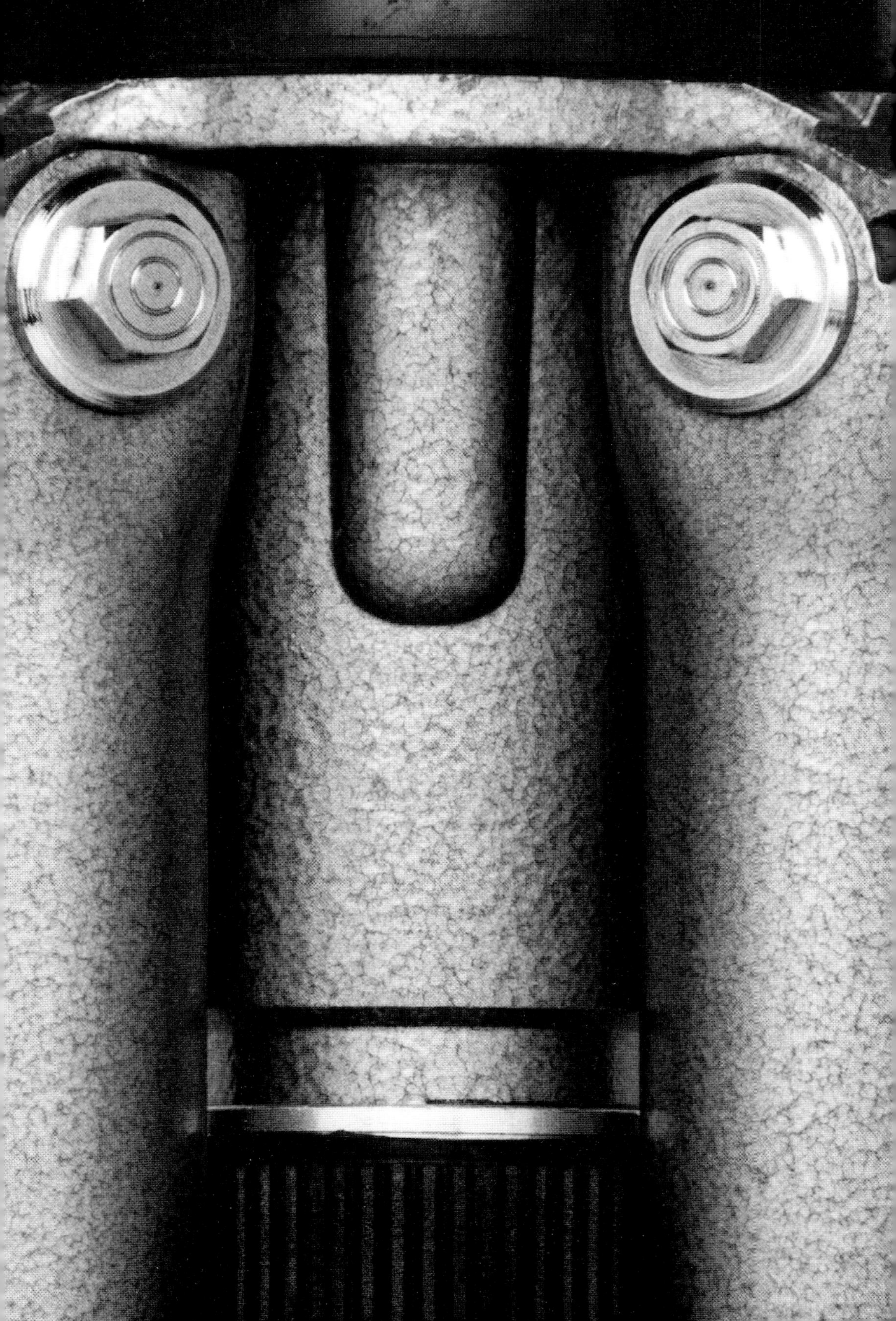

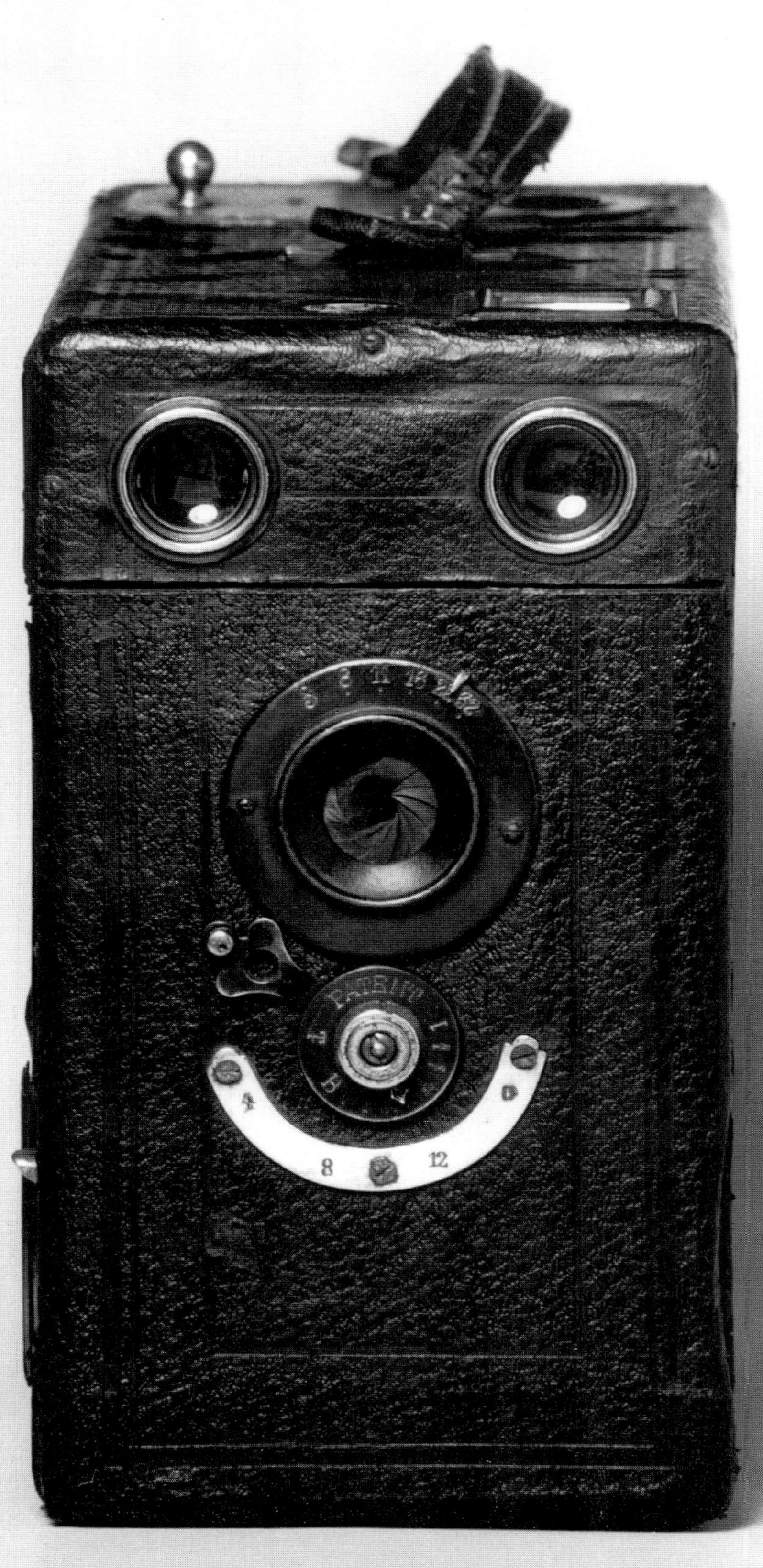
8
12

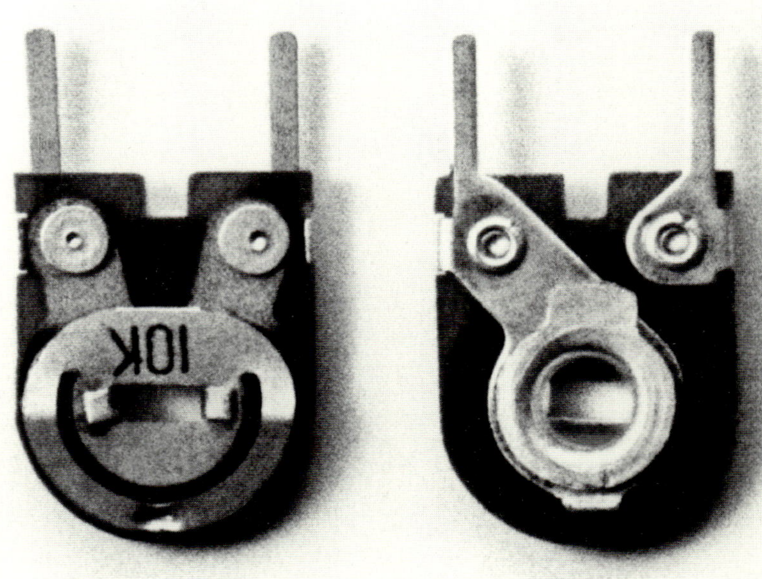
10K

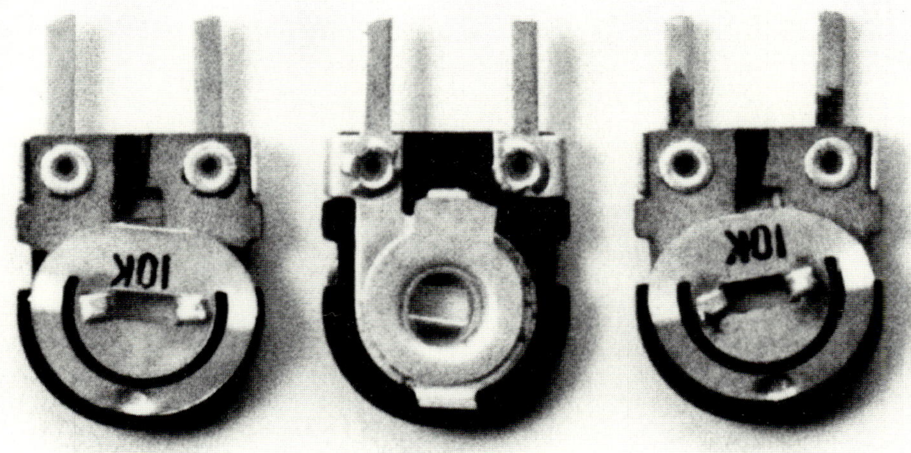
10K
10K

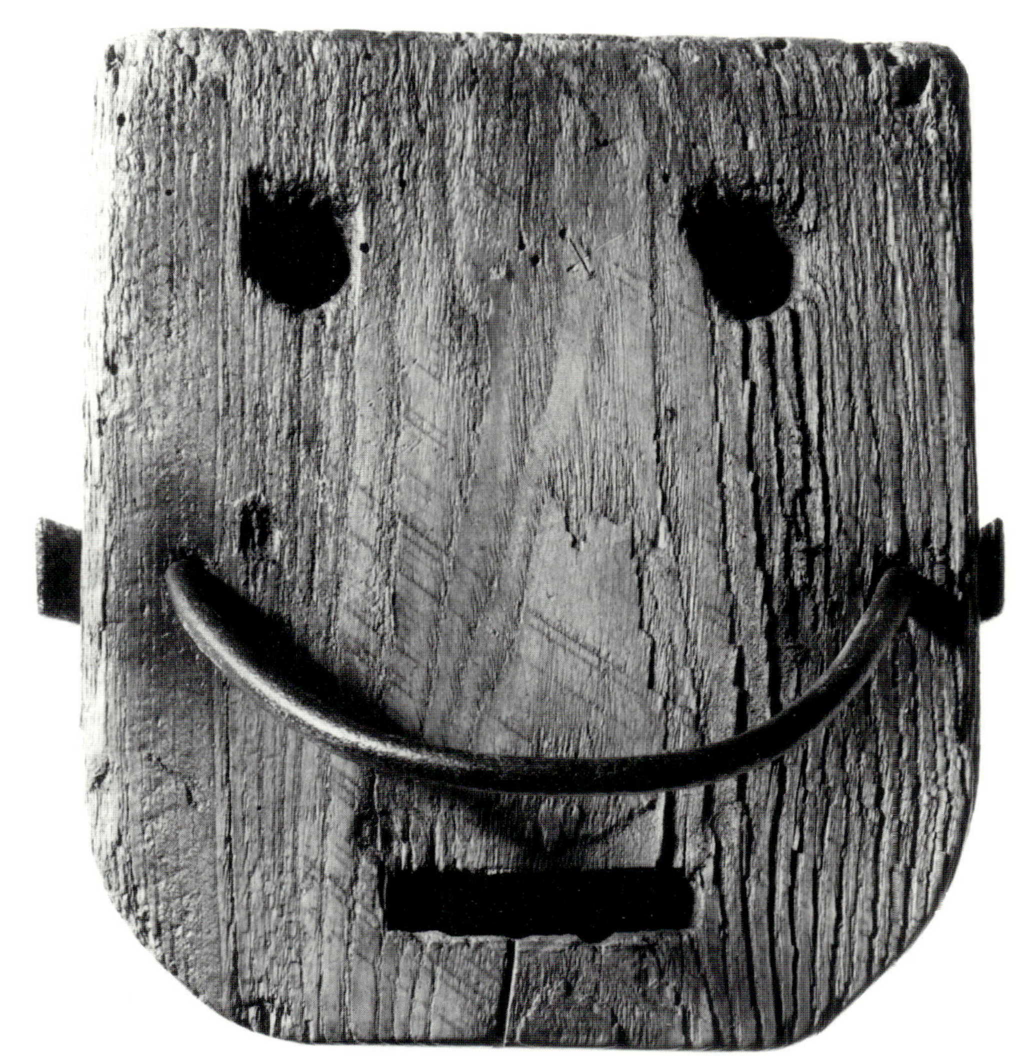

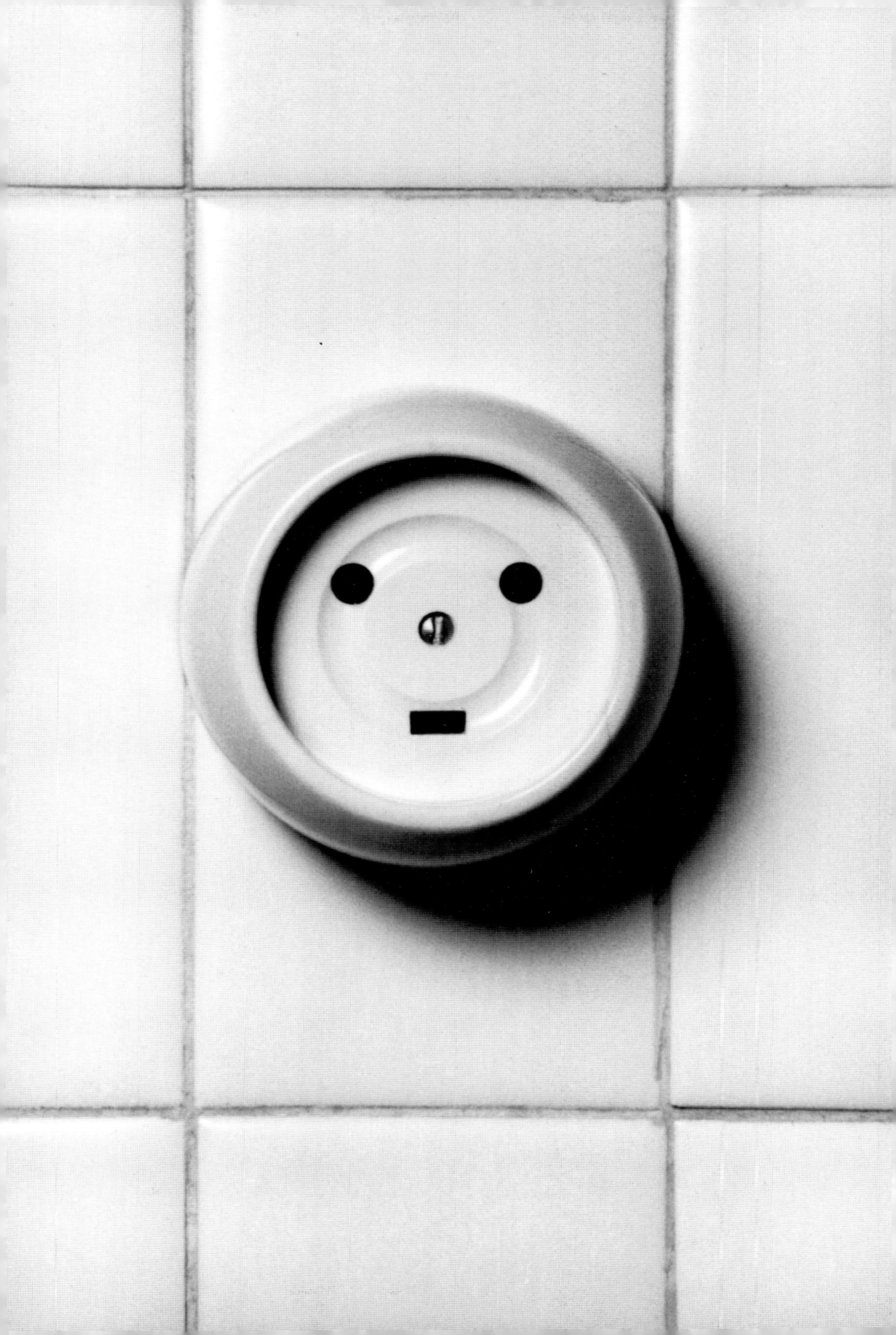

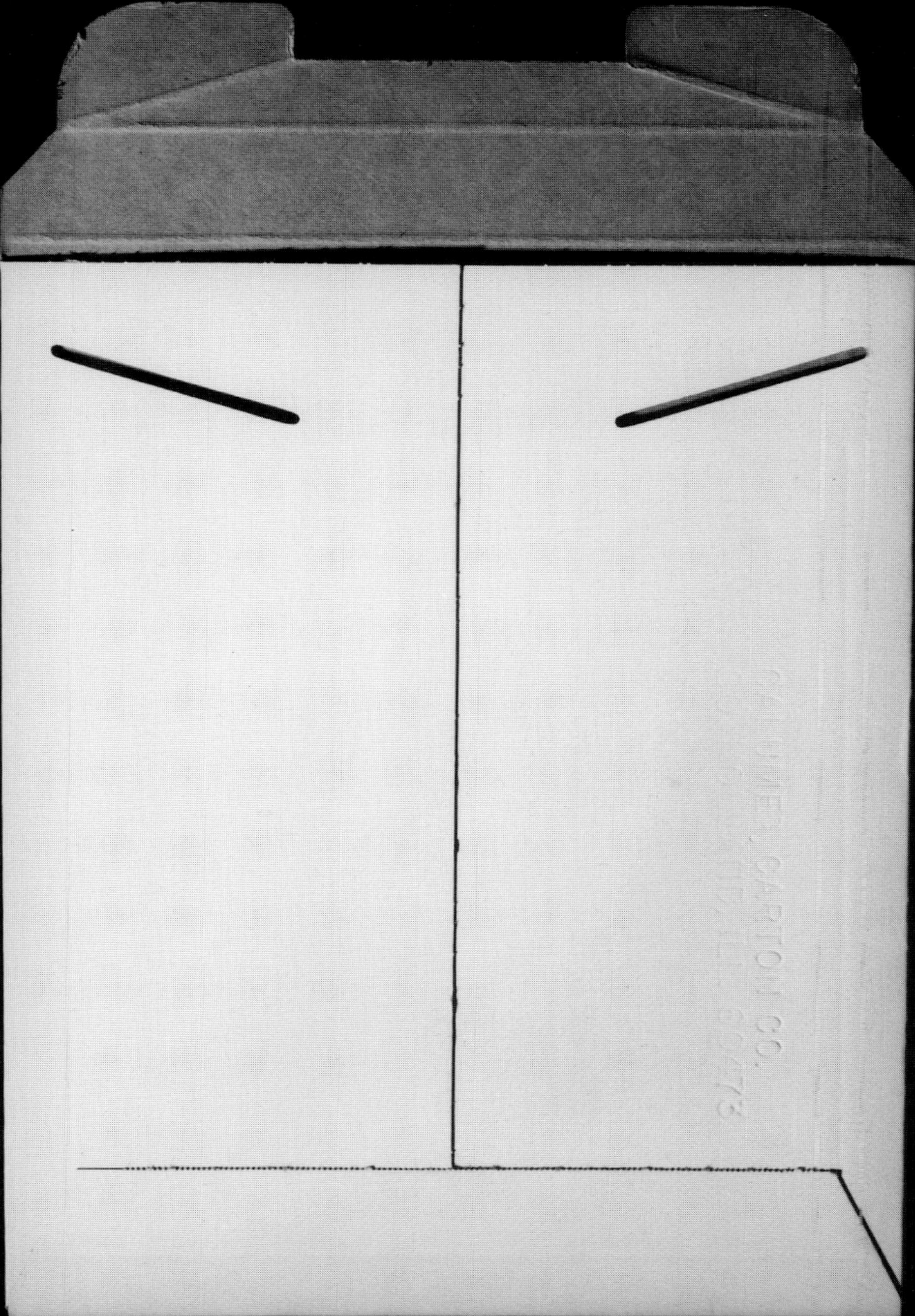

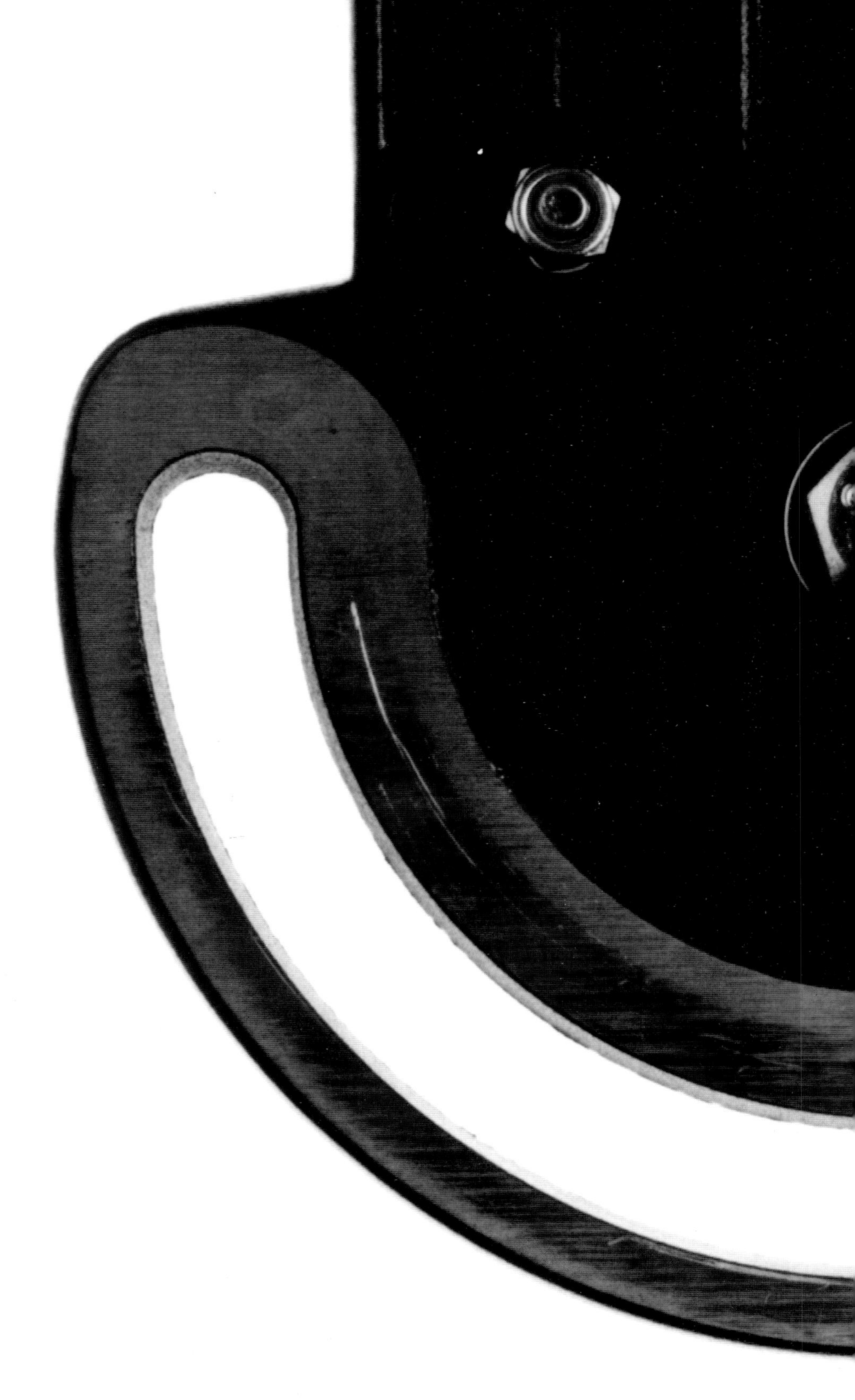

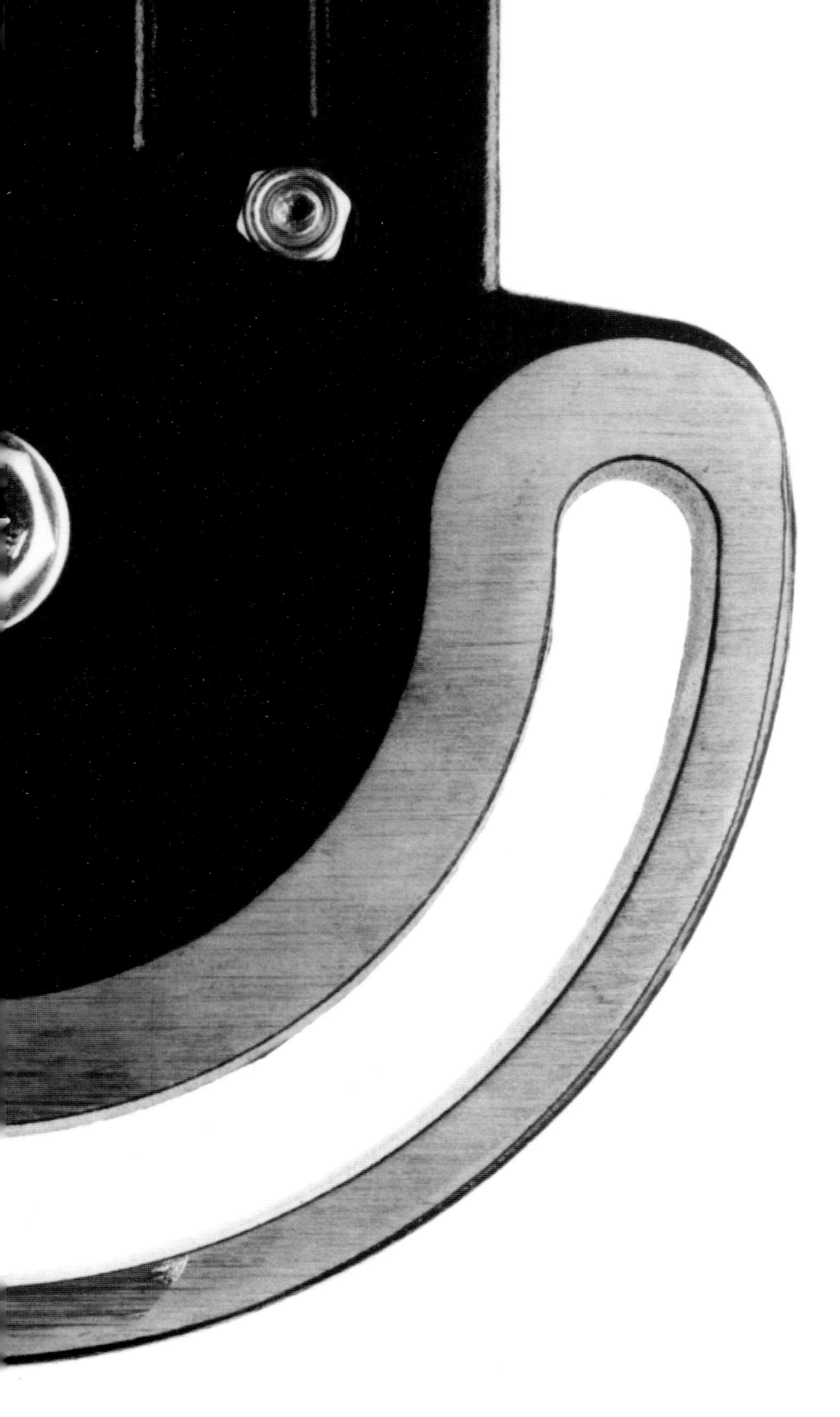

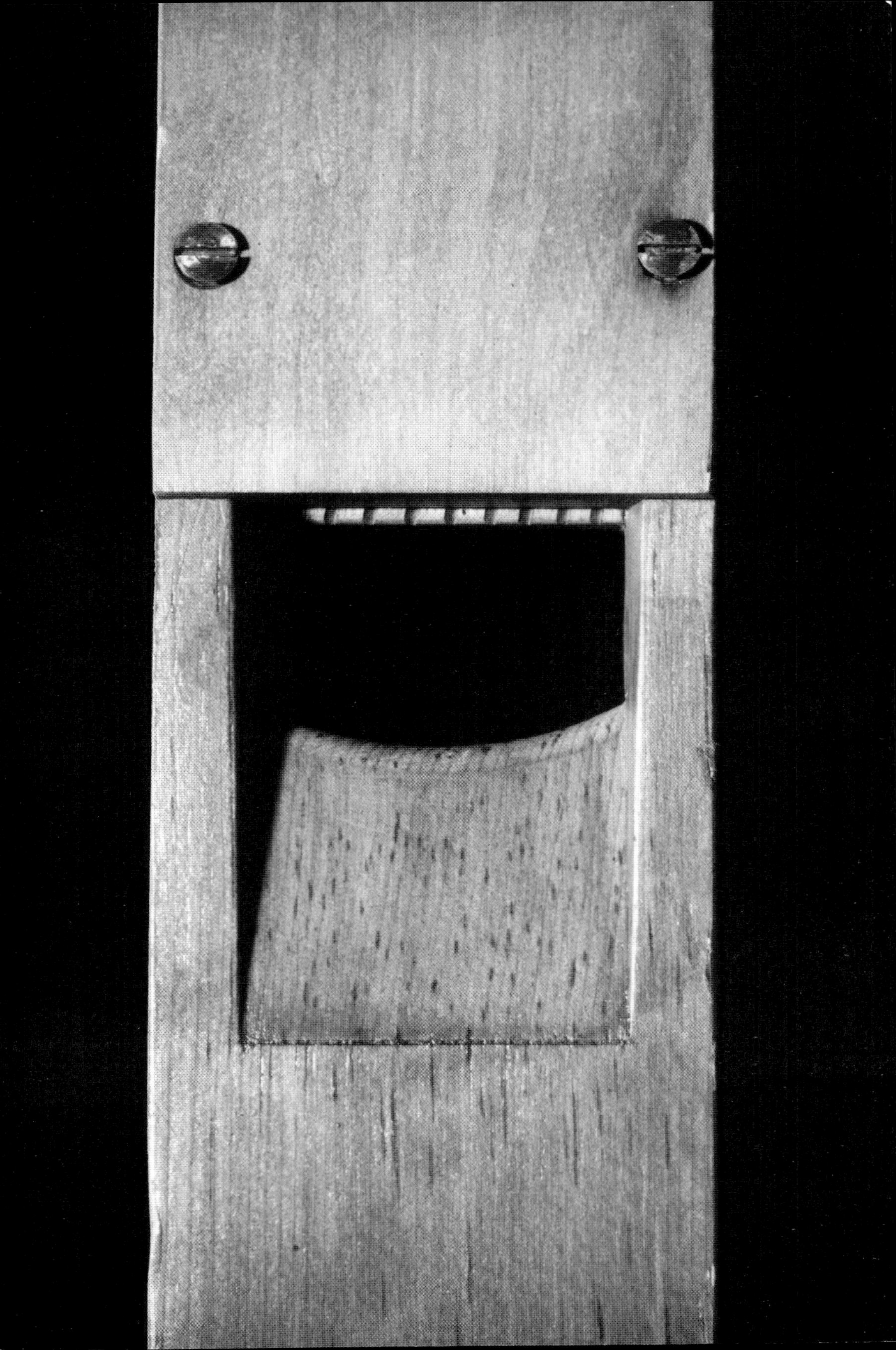

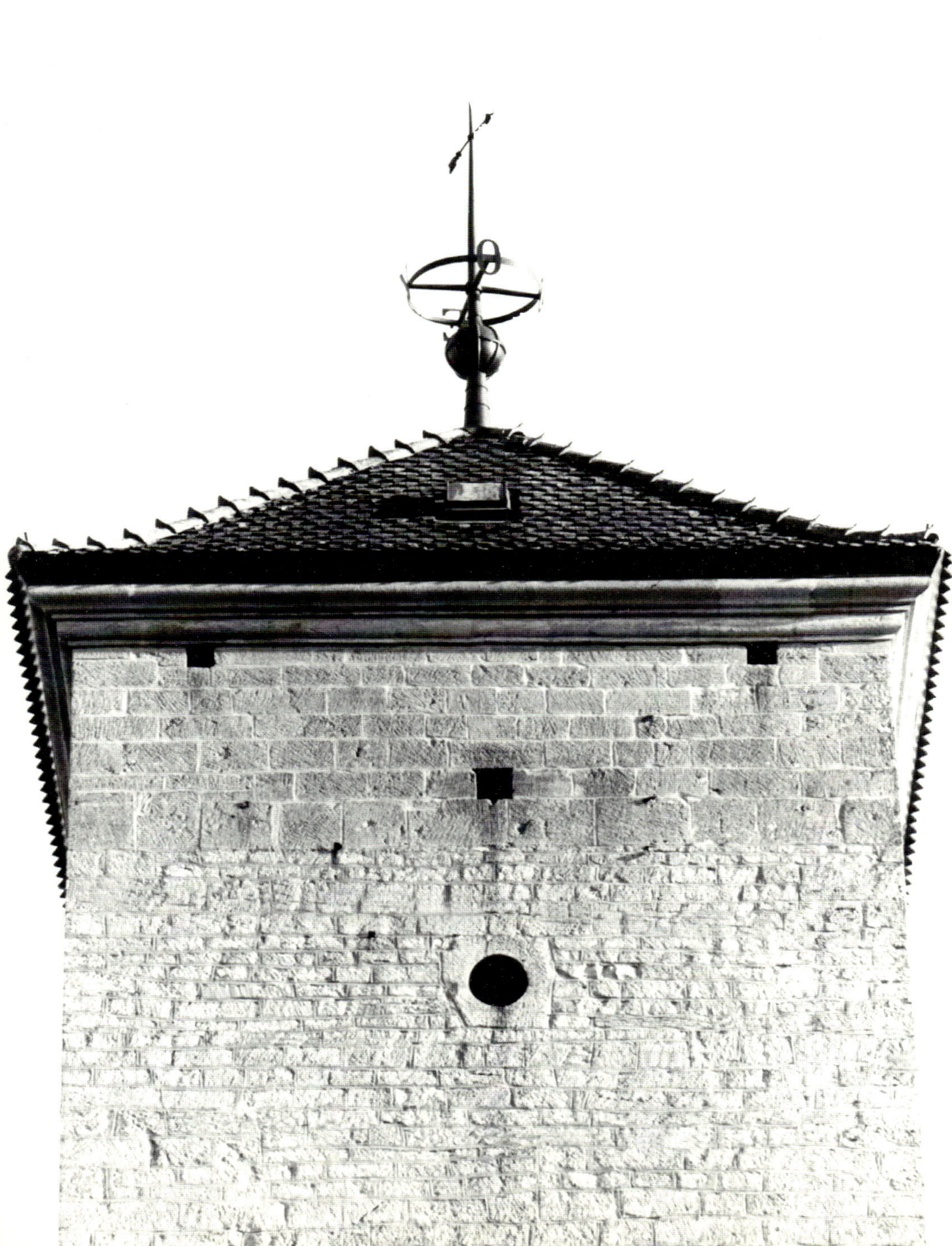

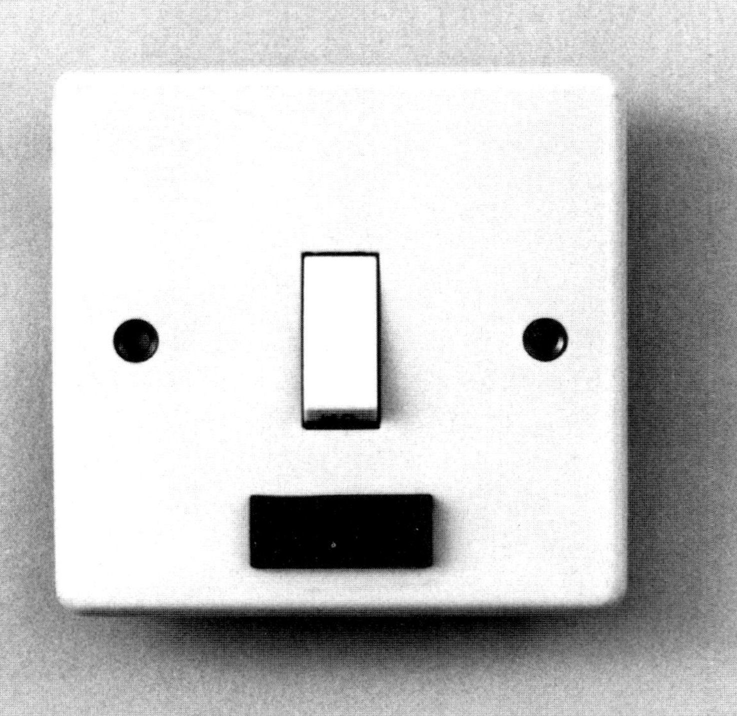

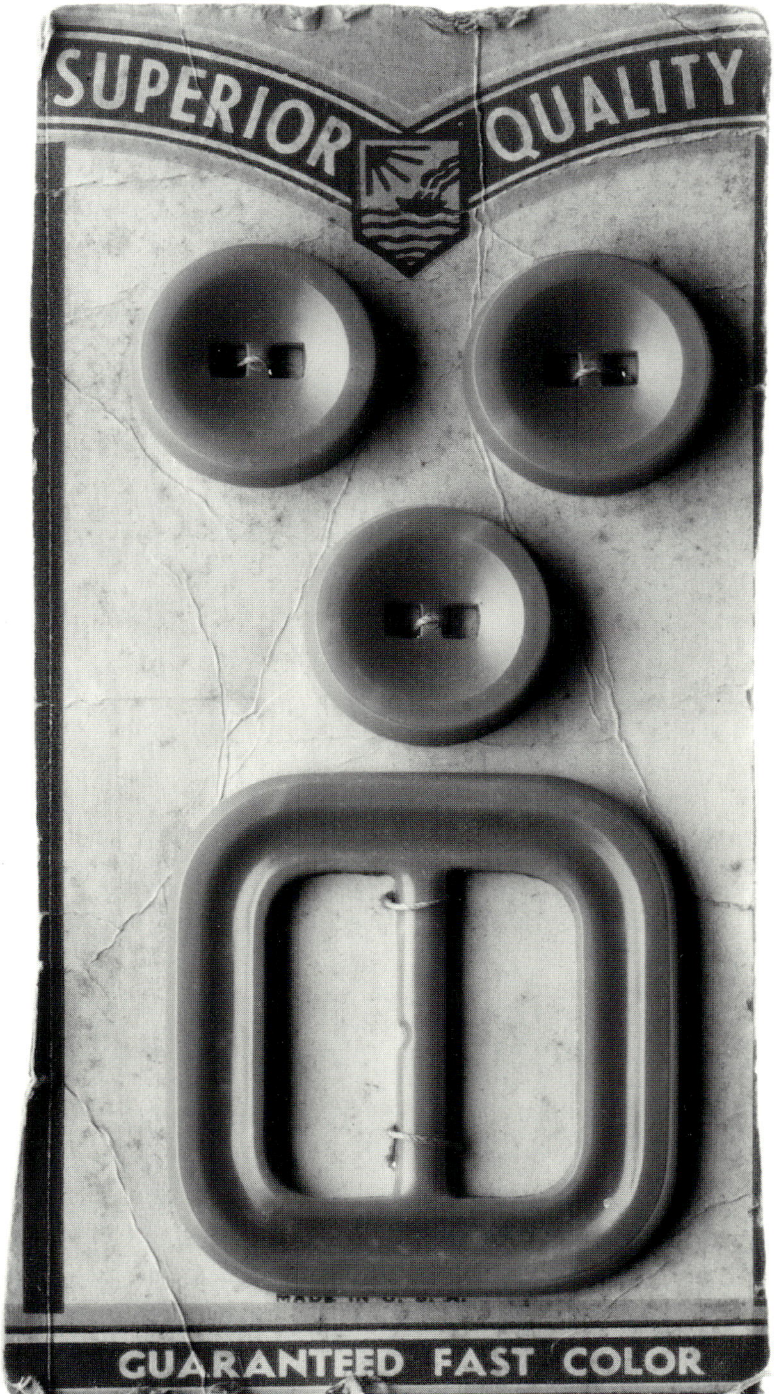

SUPERIOR QUALITY

GUARANTEED FAST COLOR

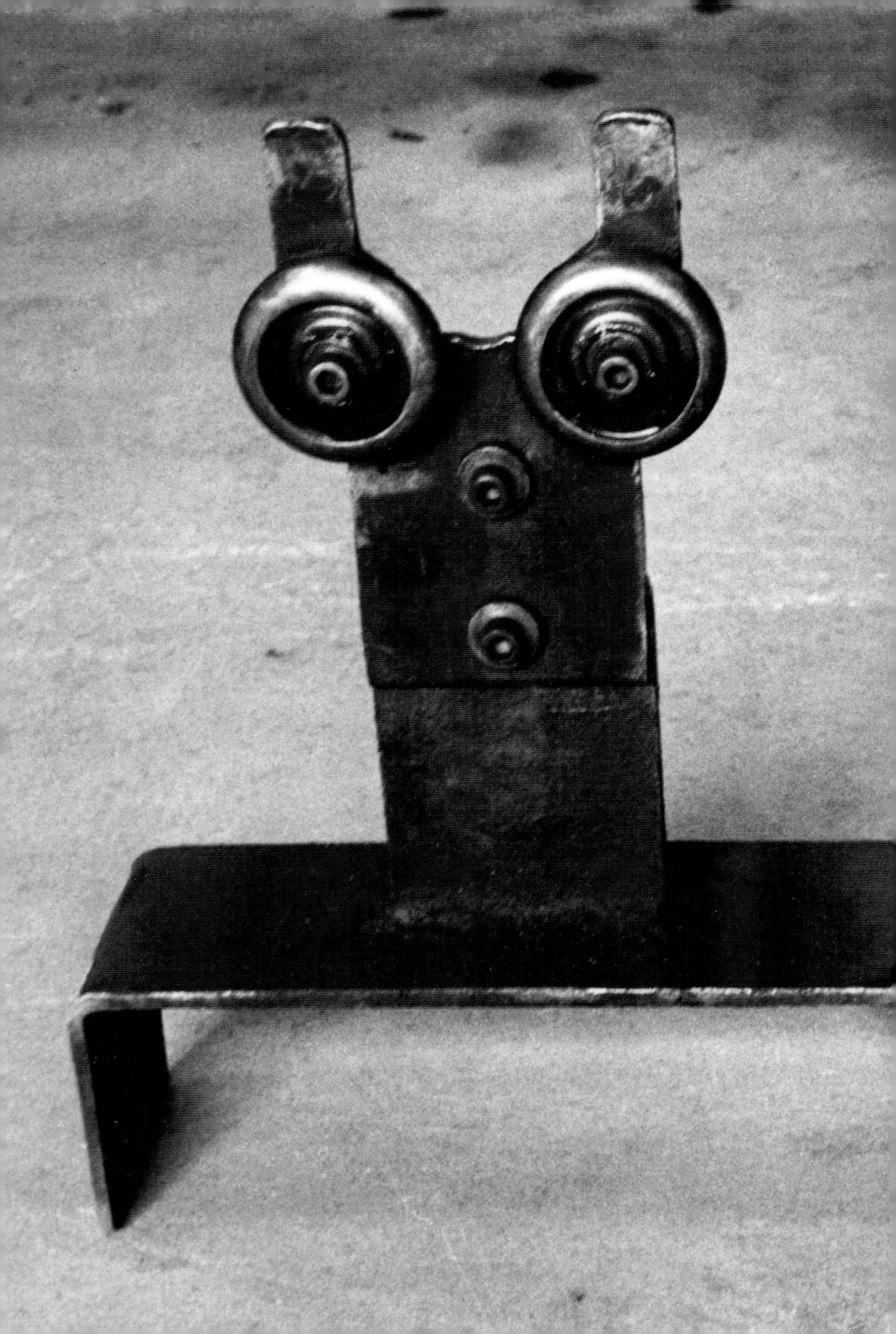

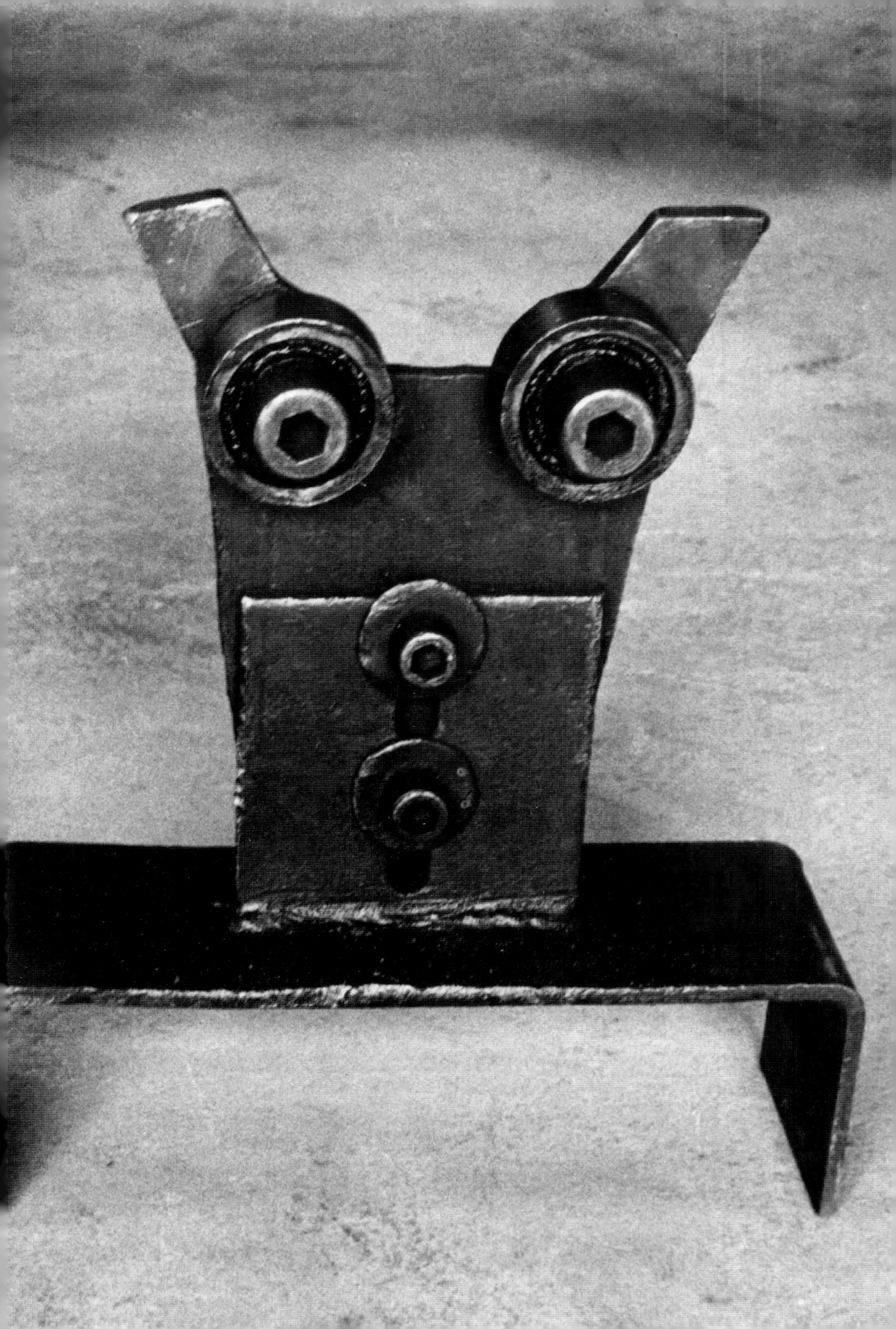

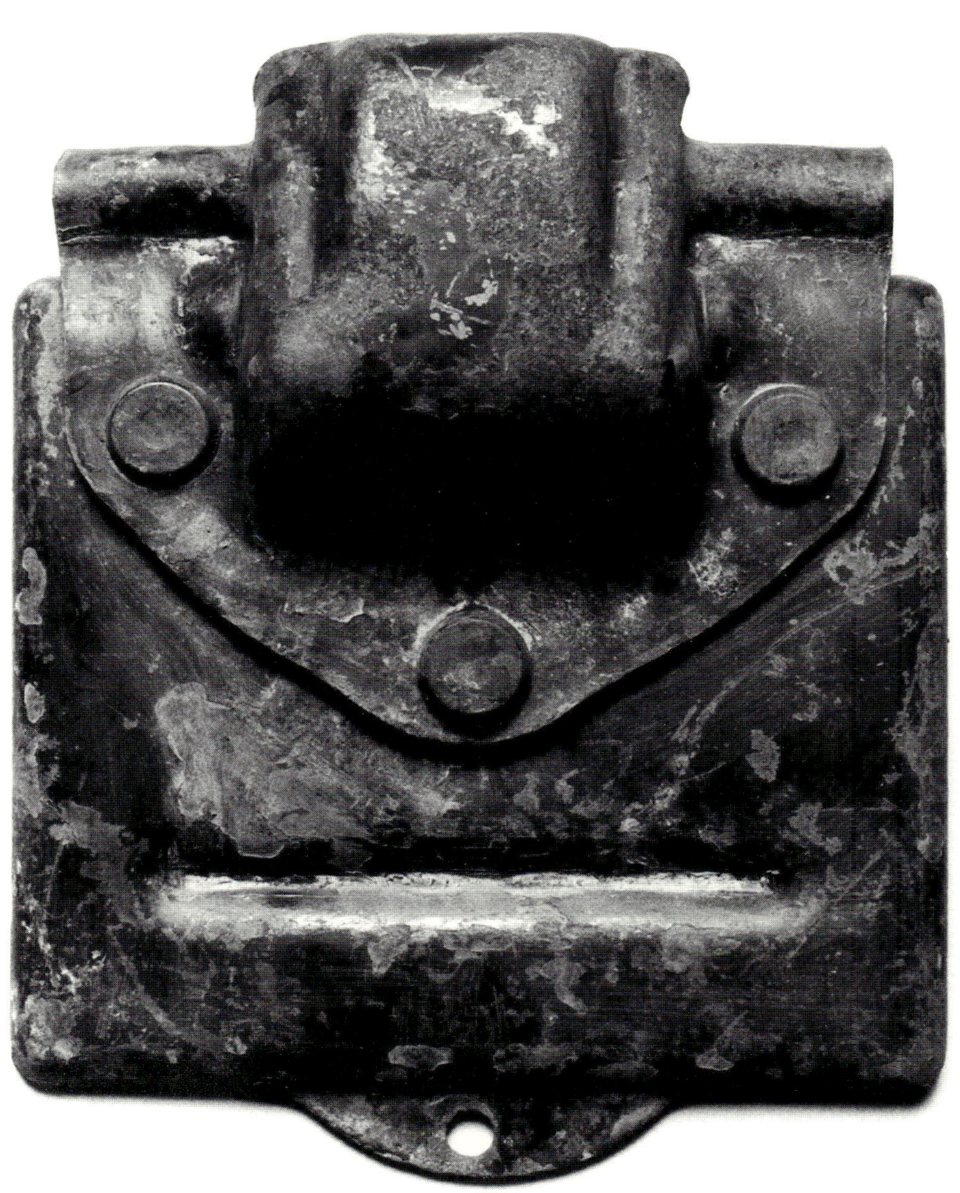

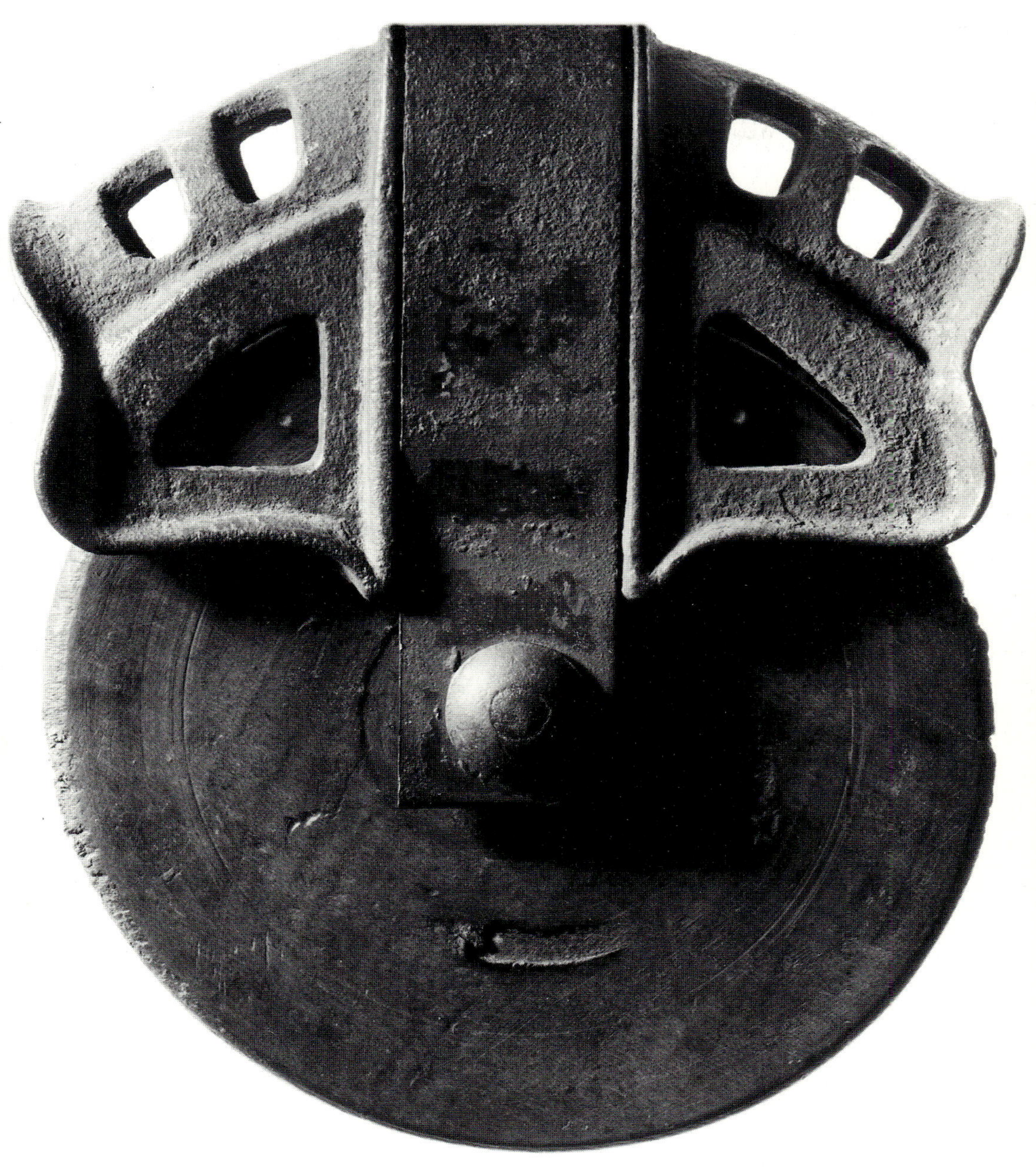

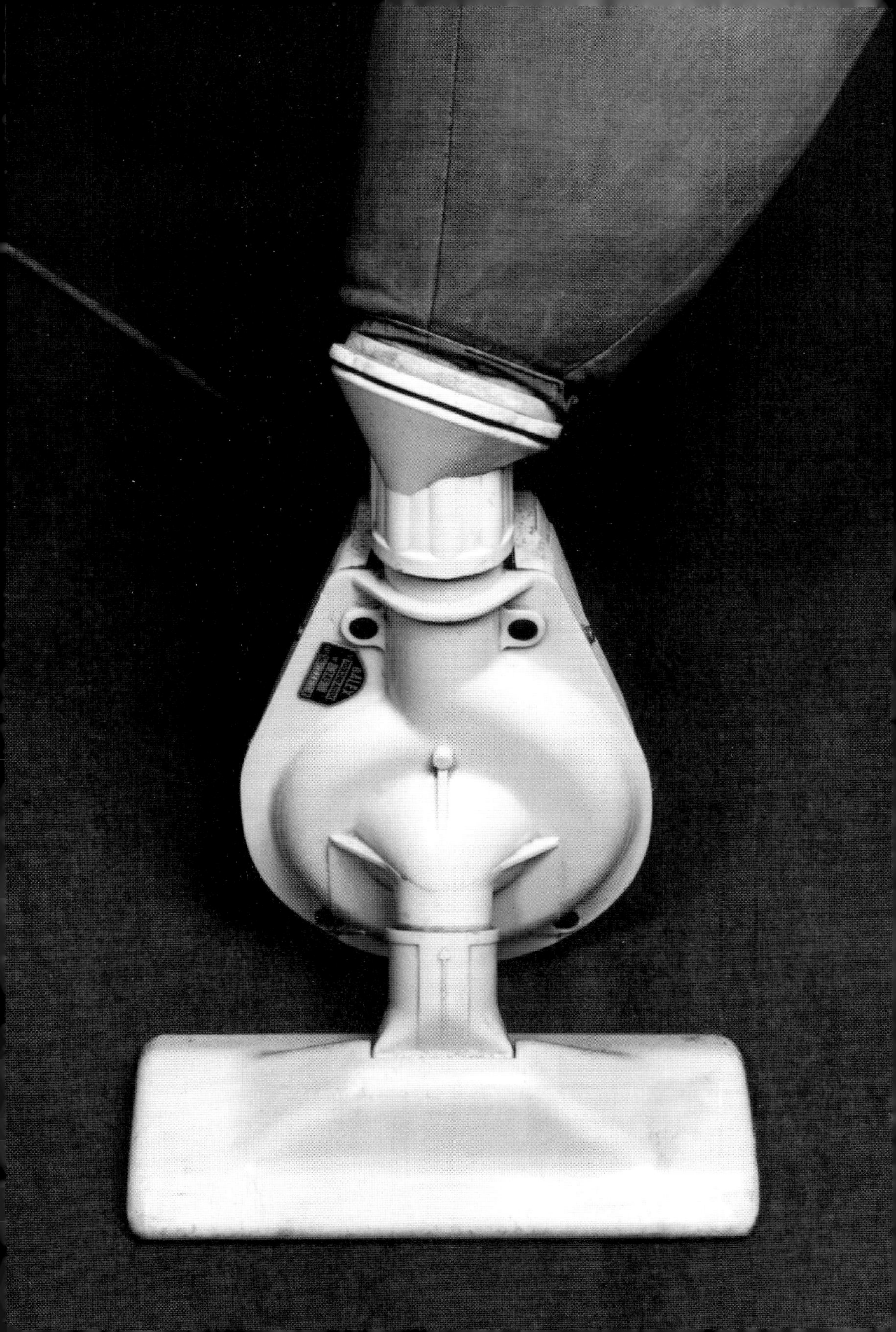

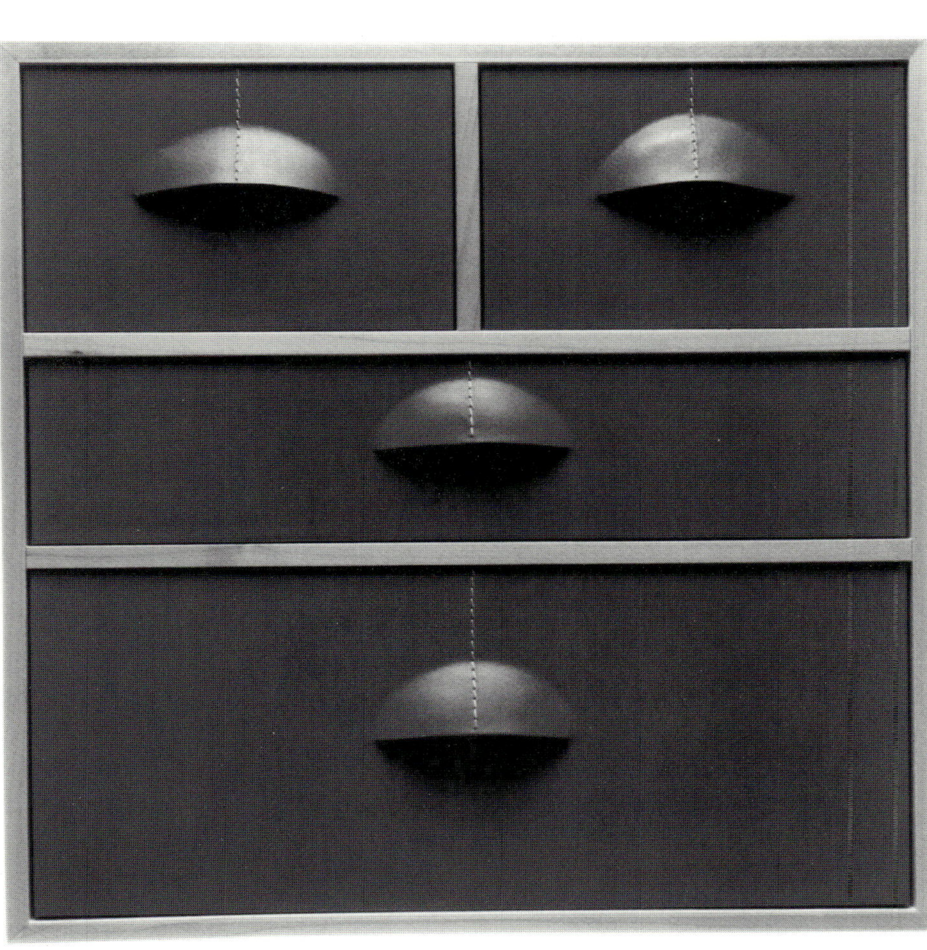

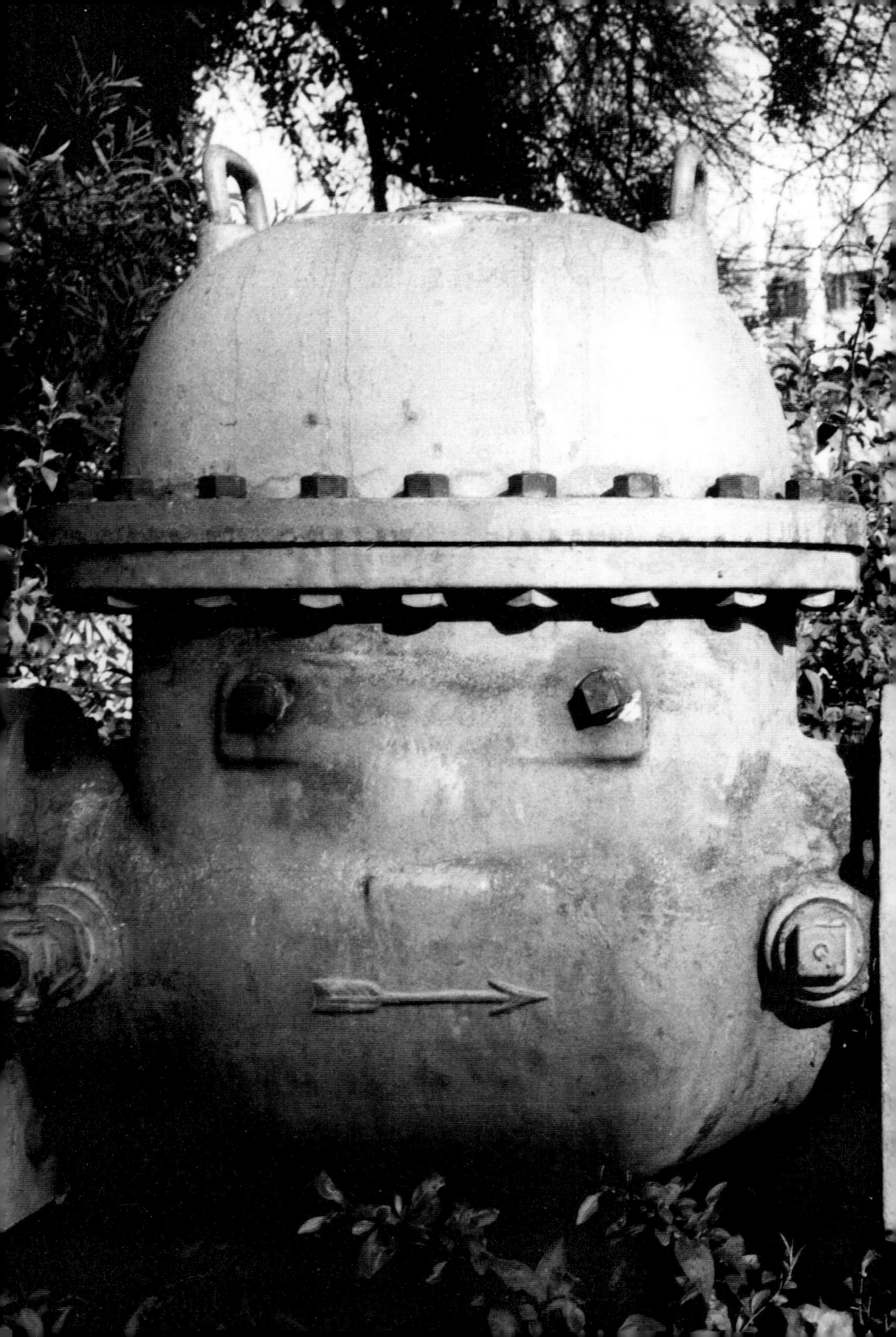

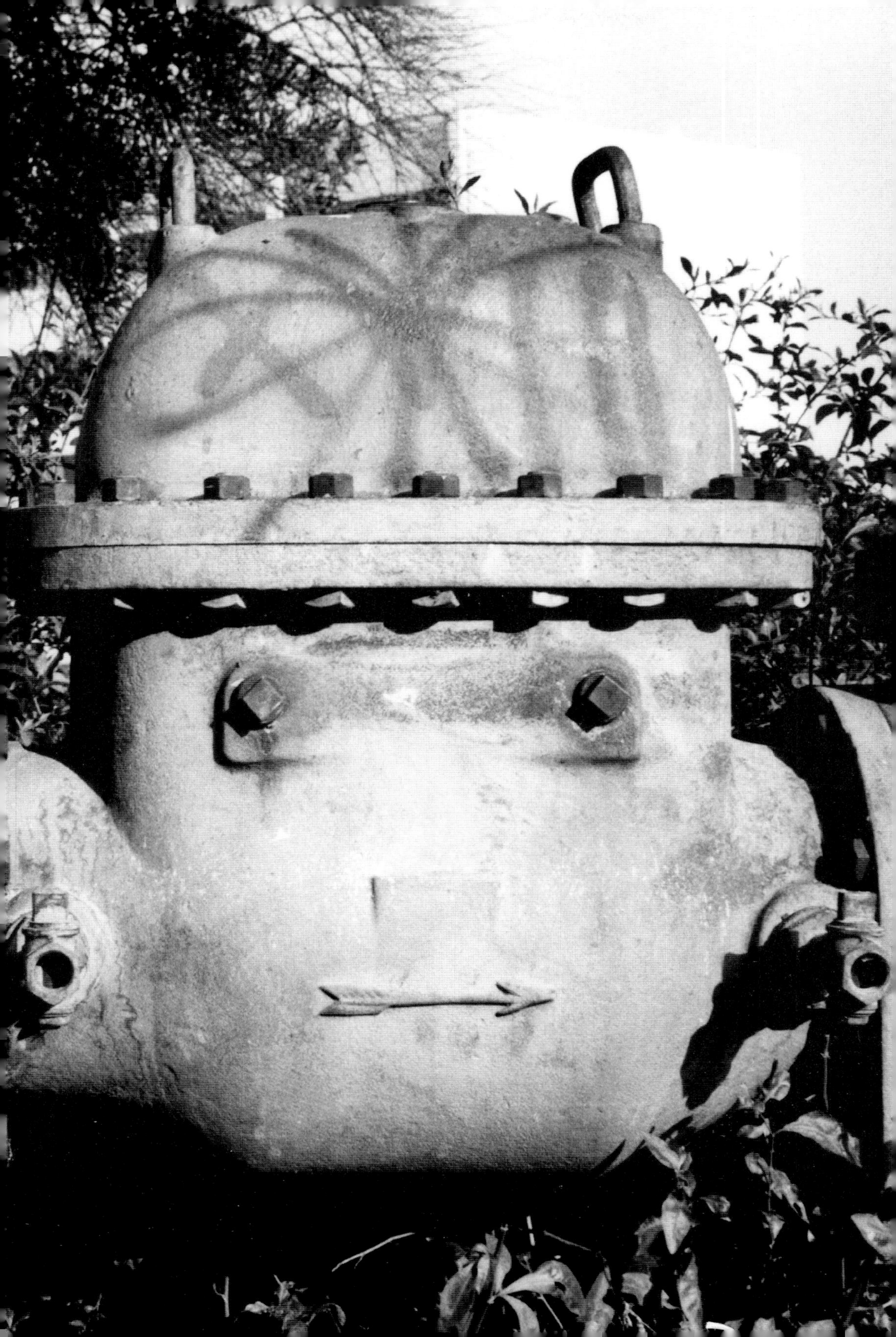

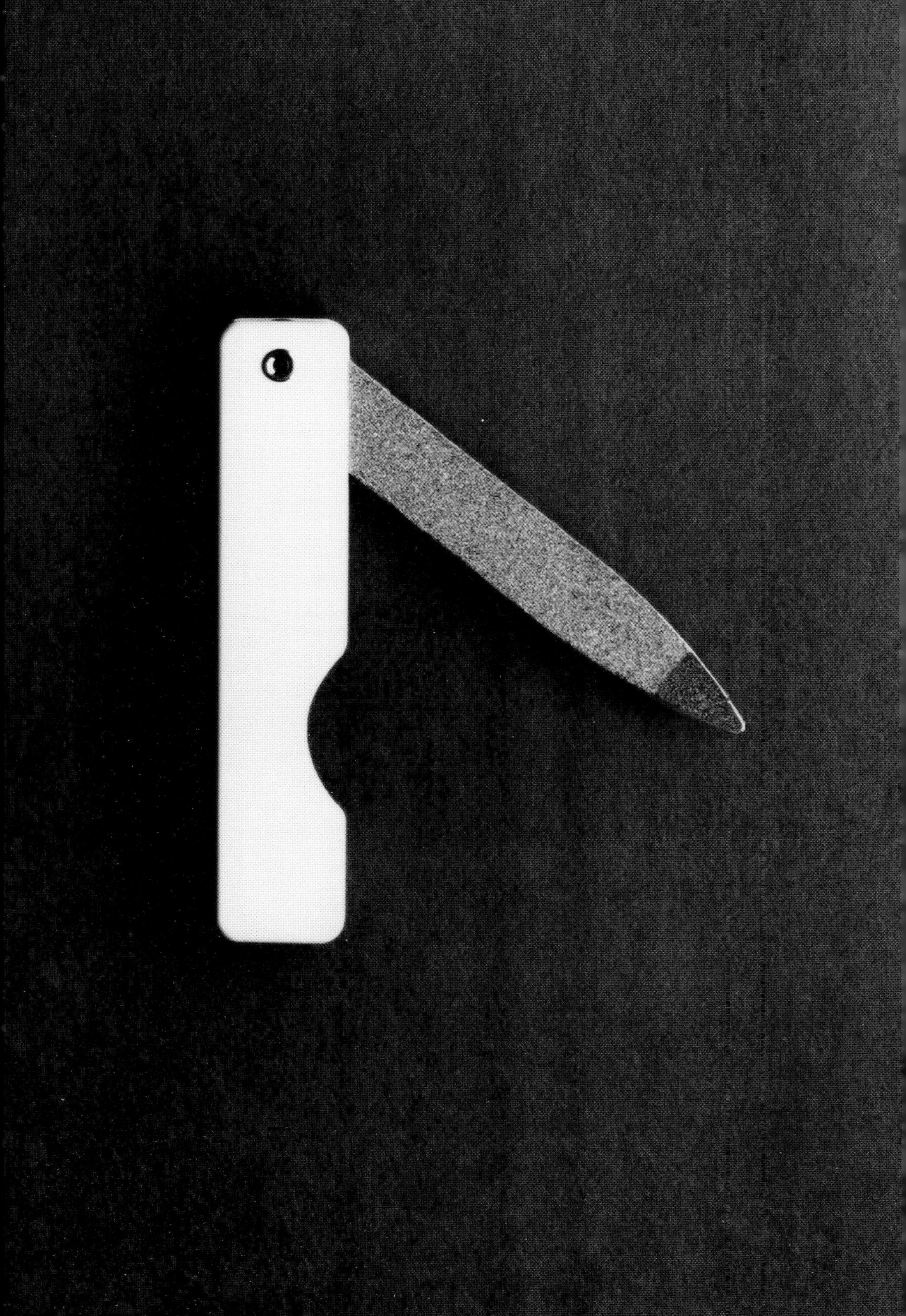

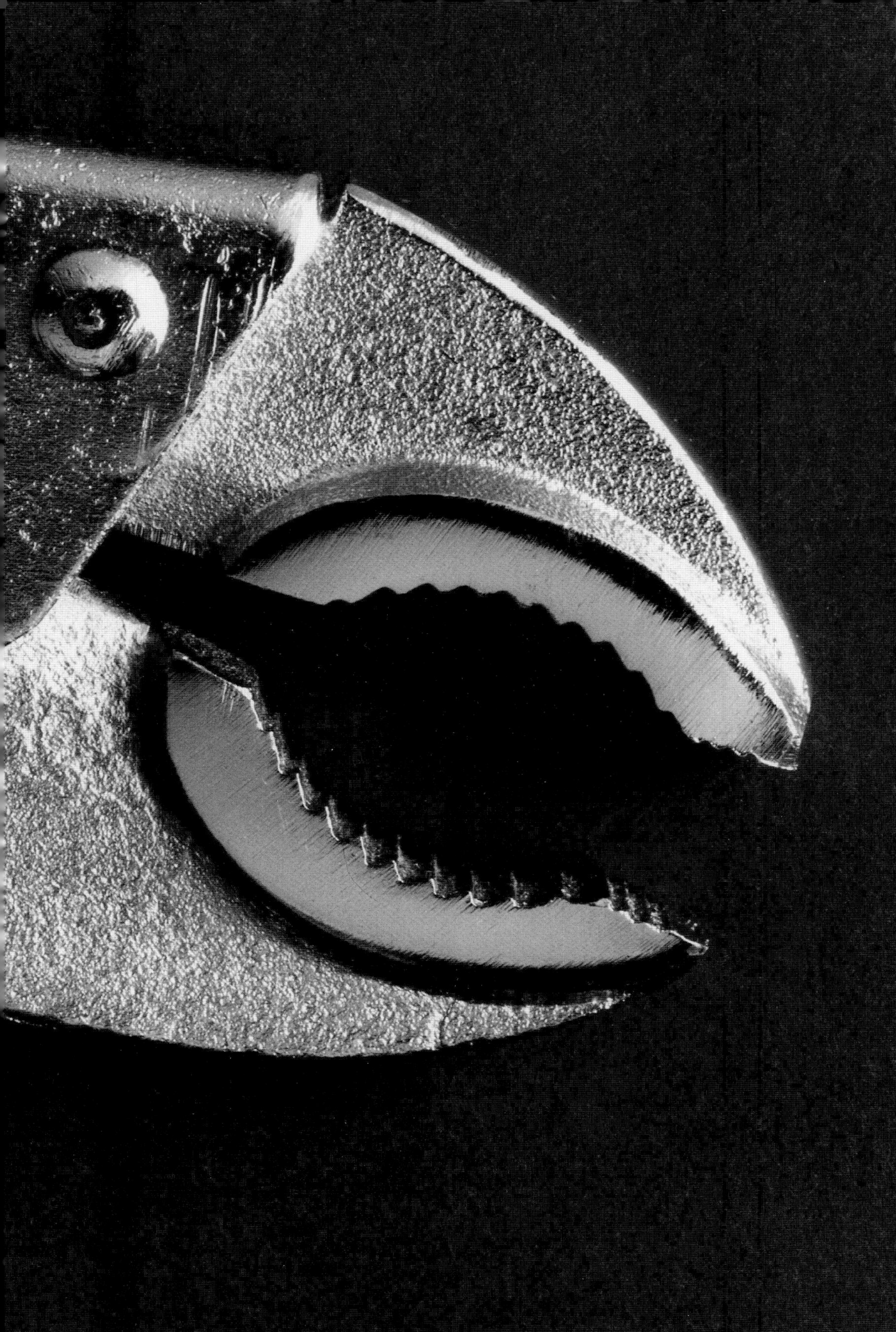

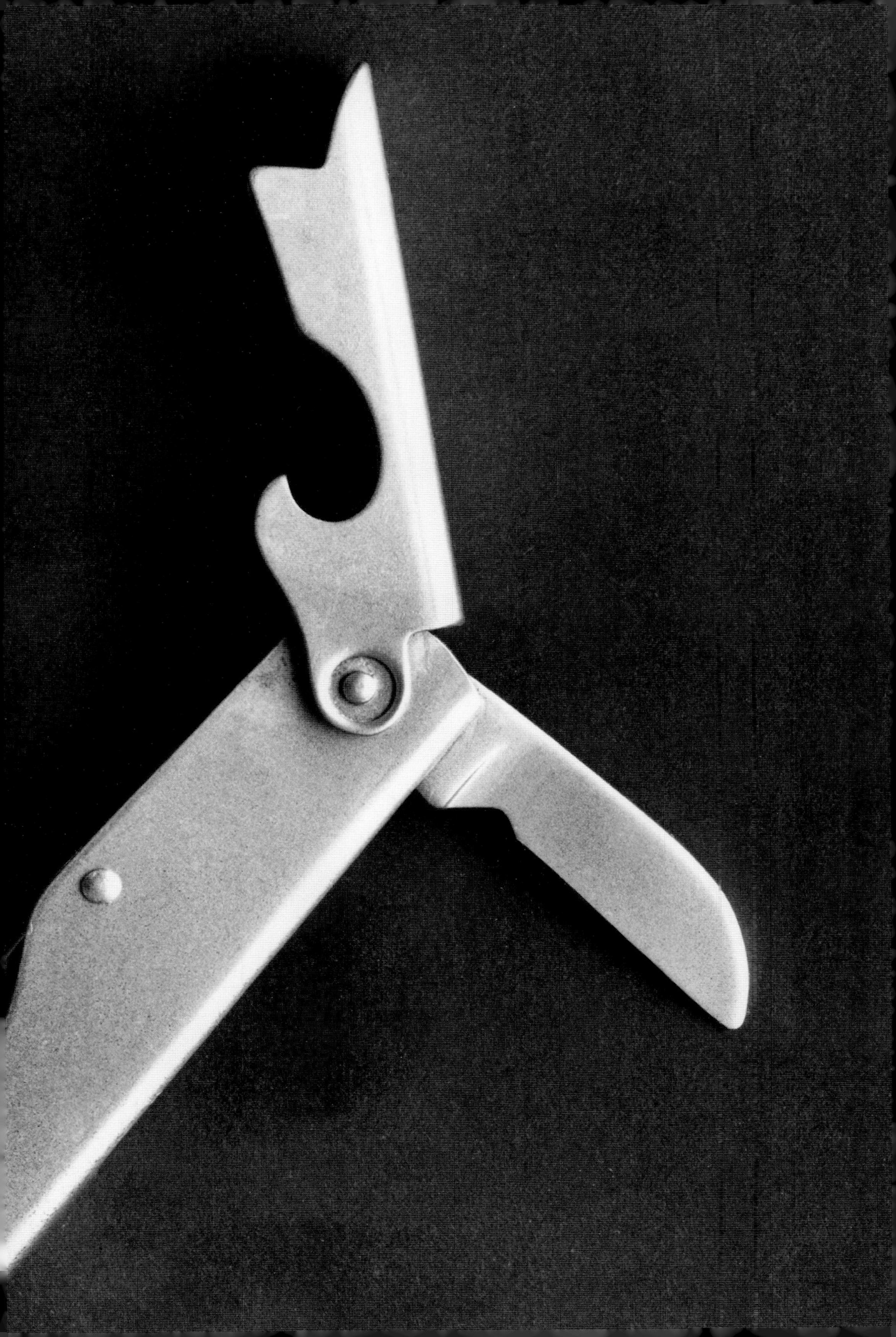

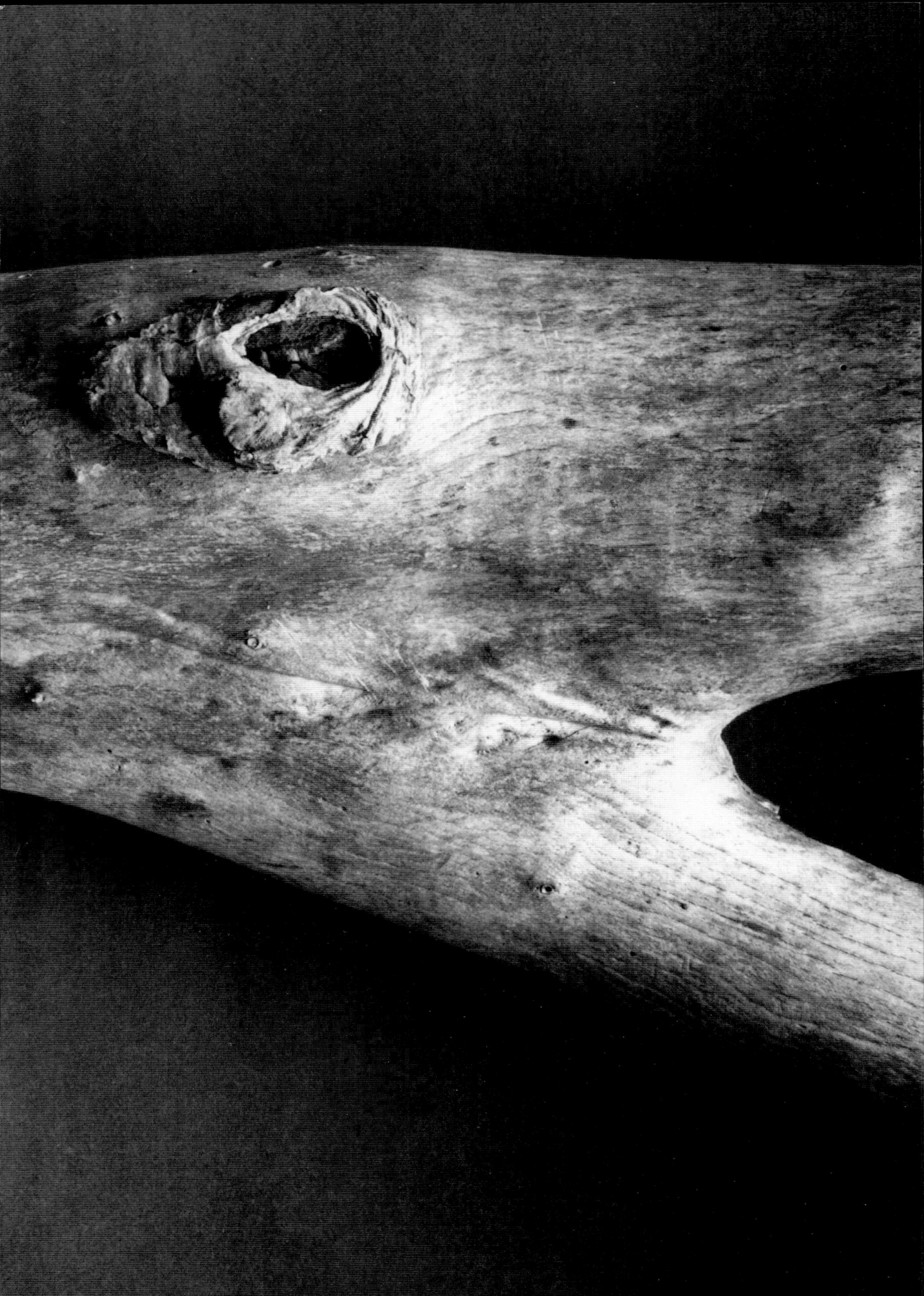

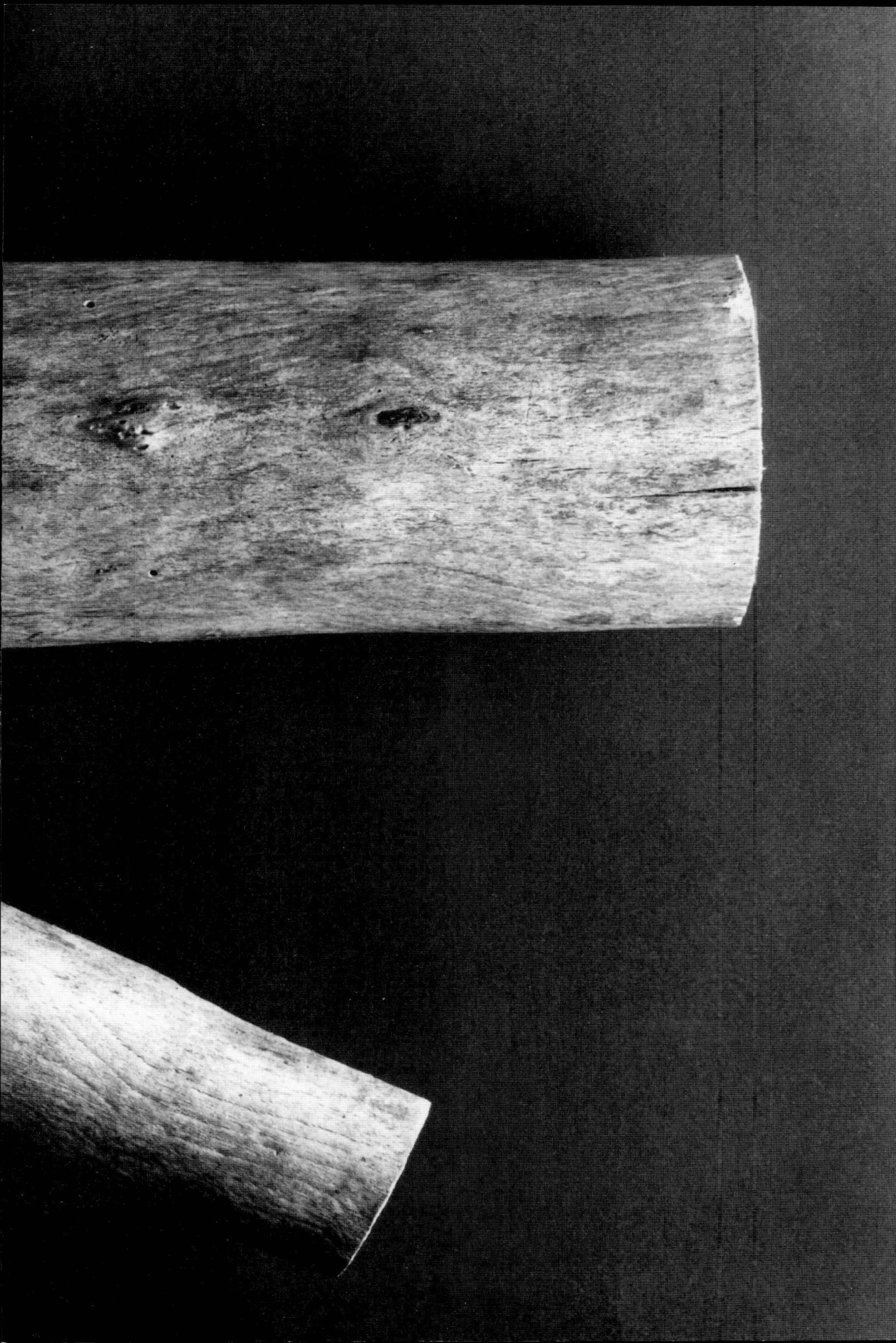

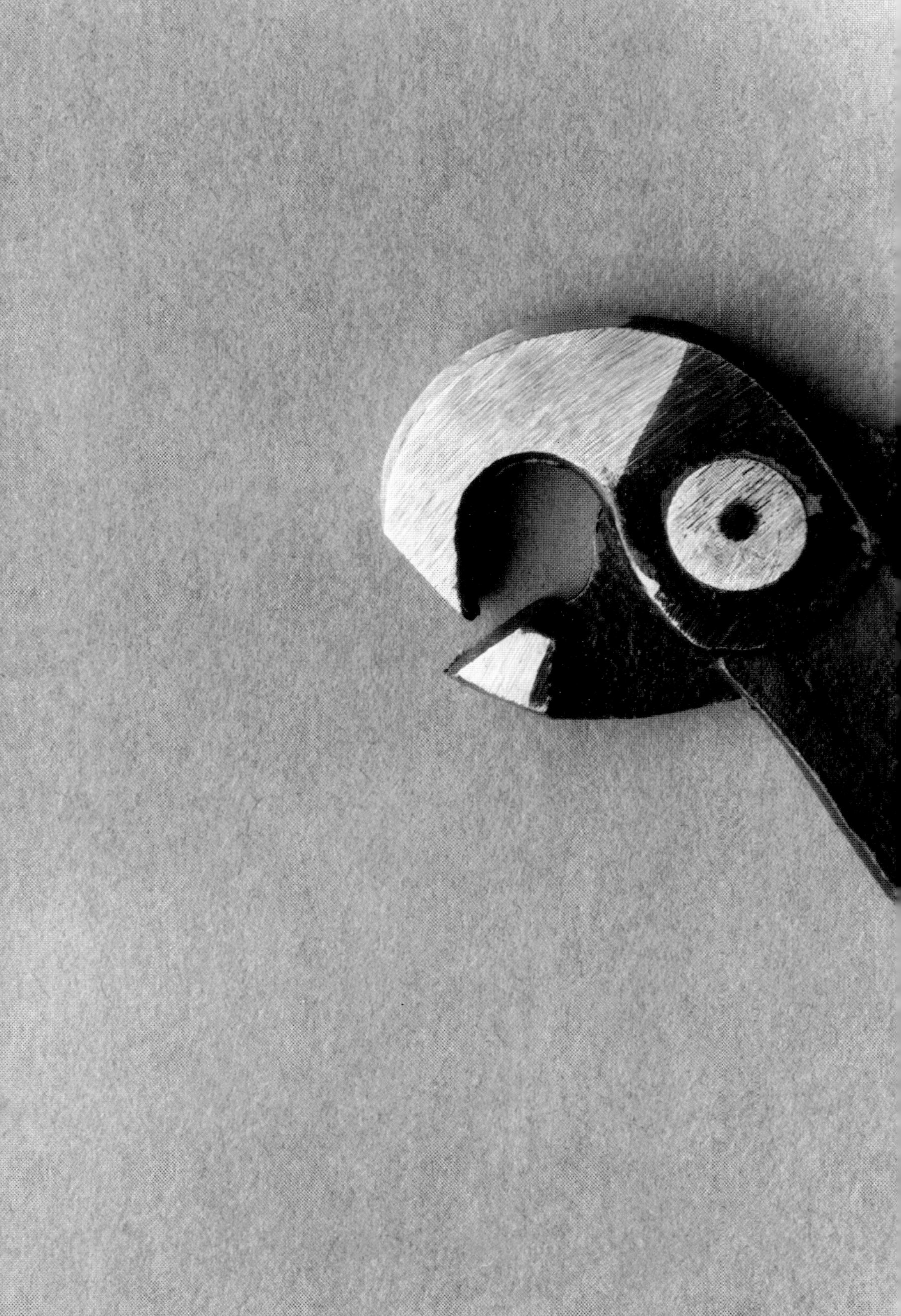

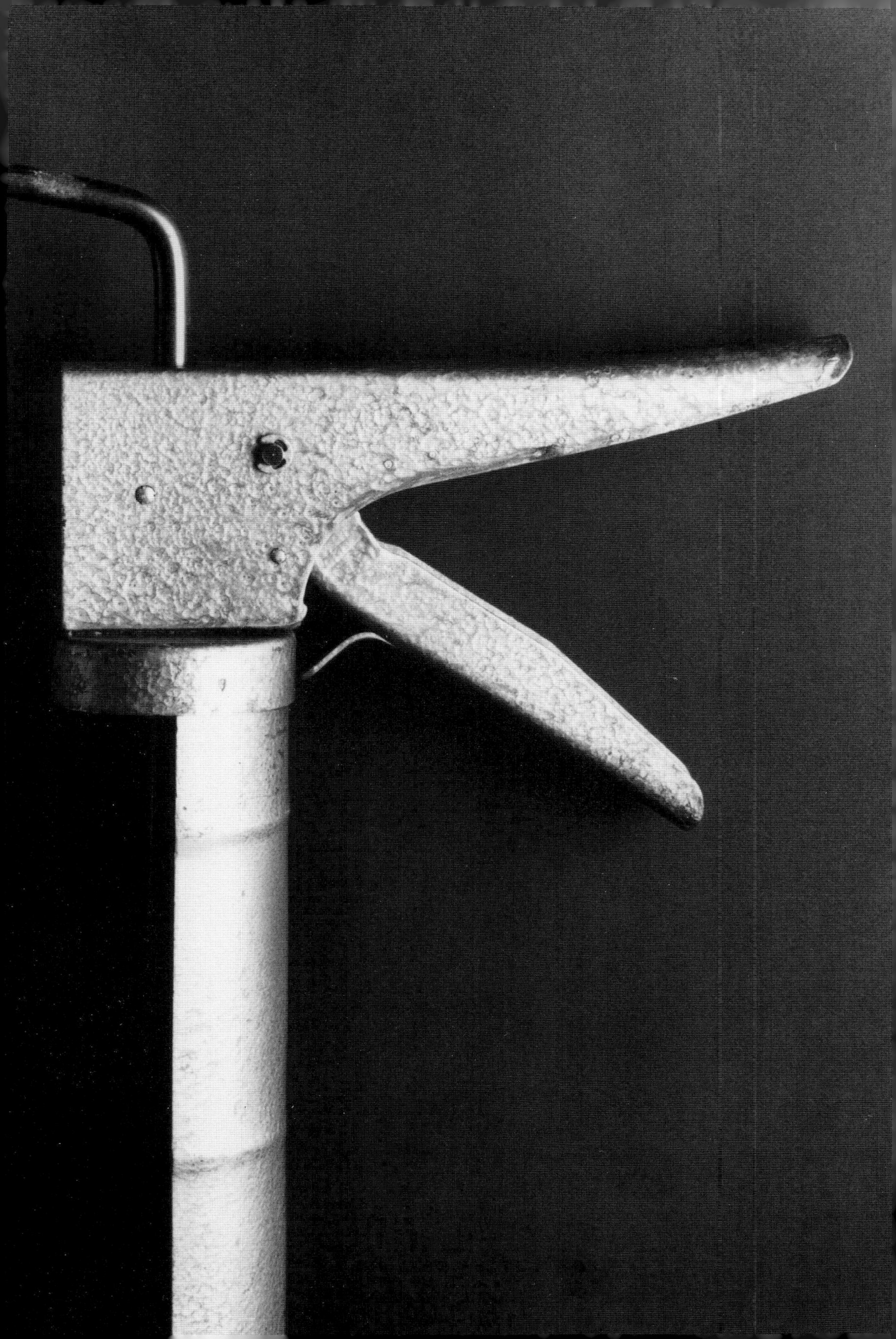

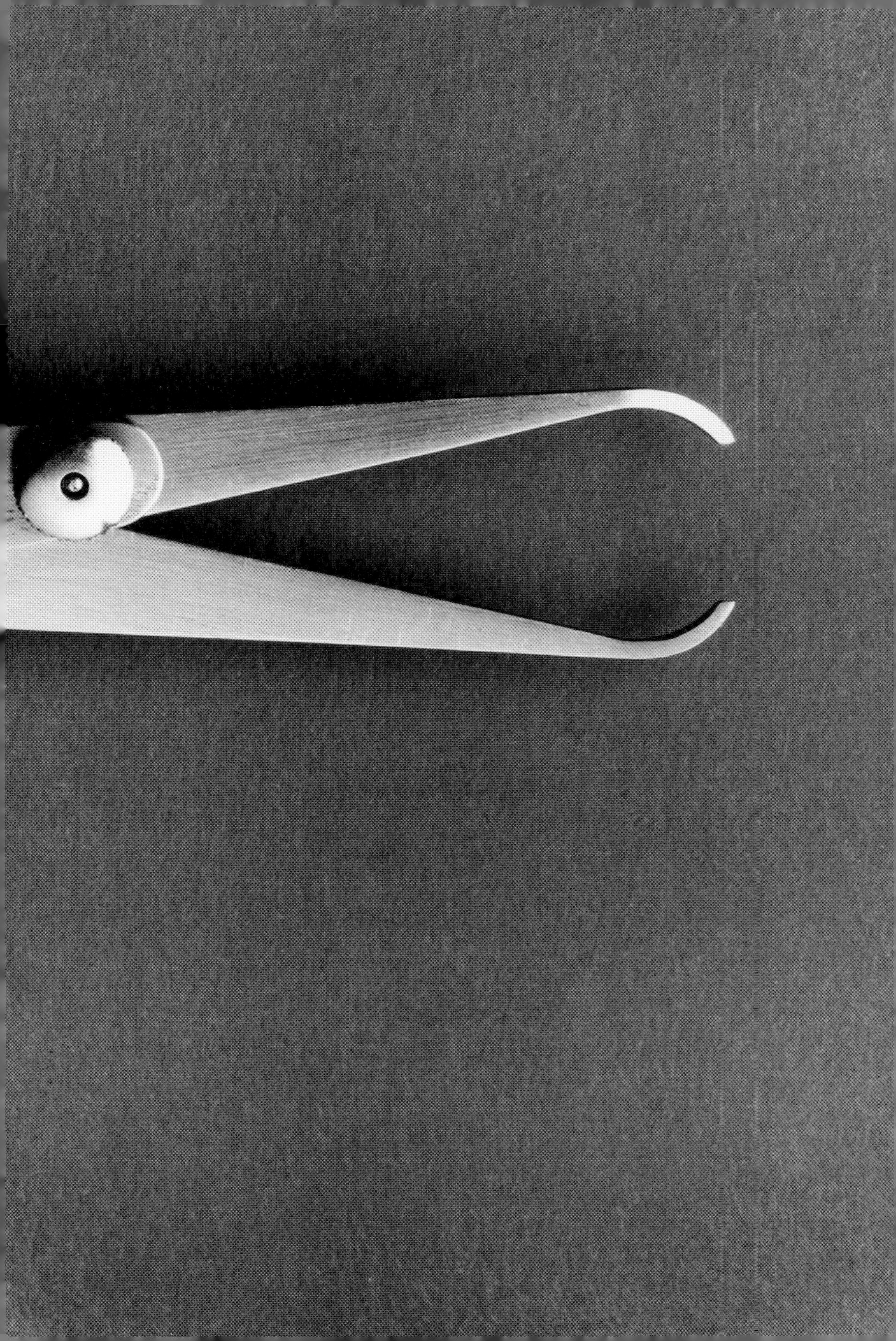

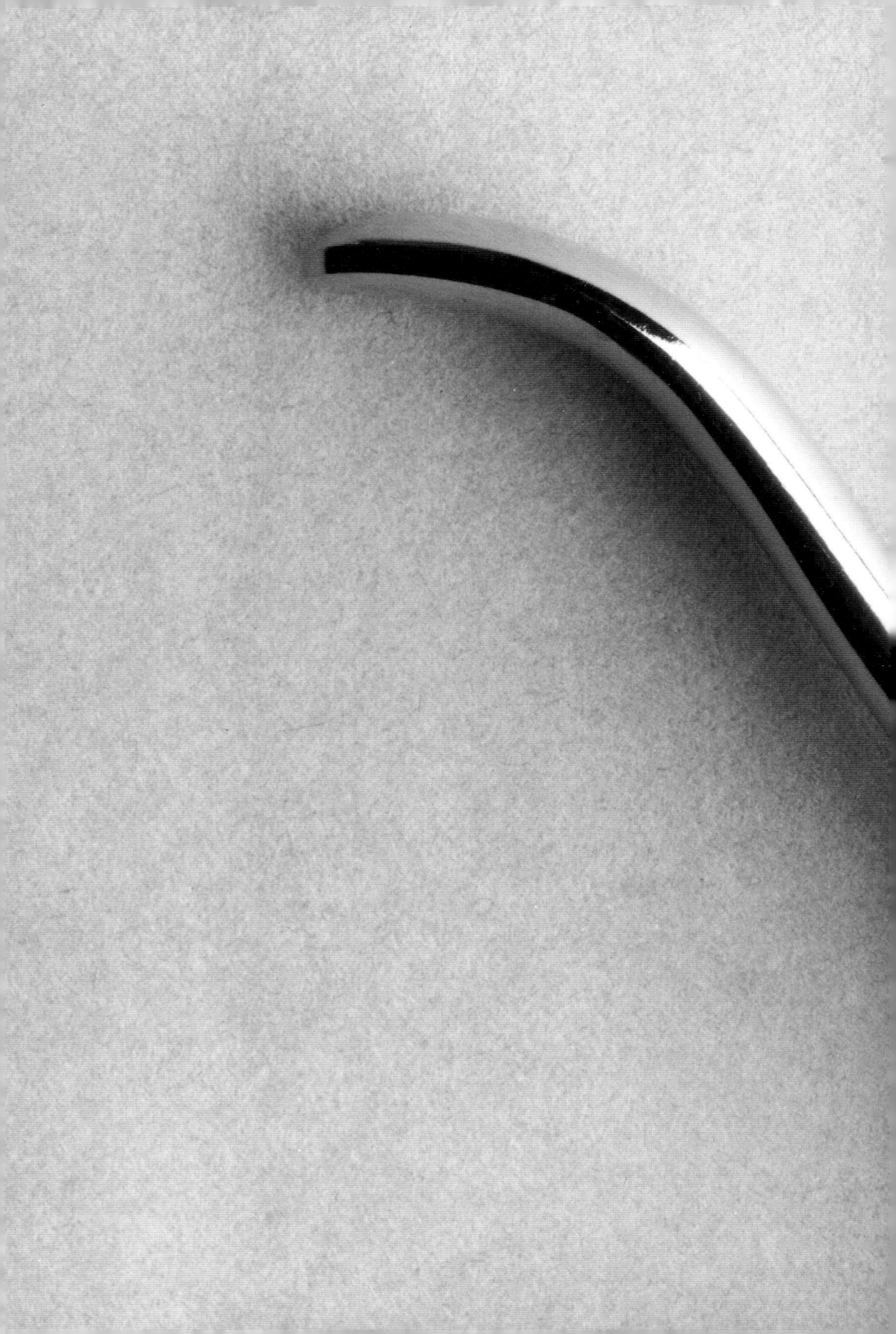

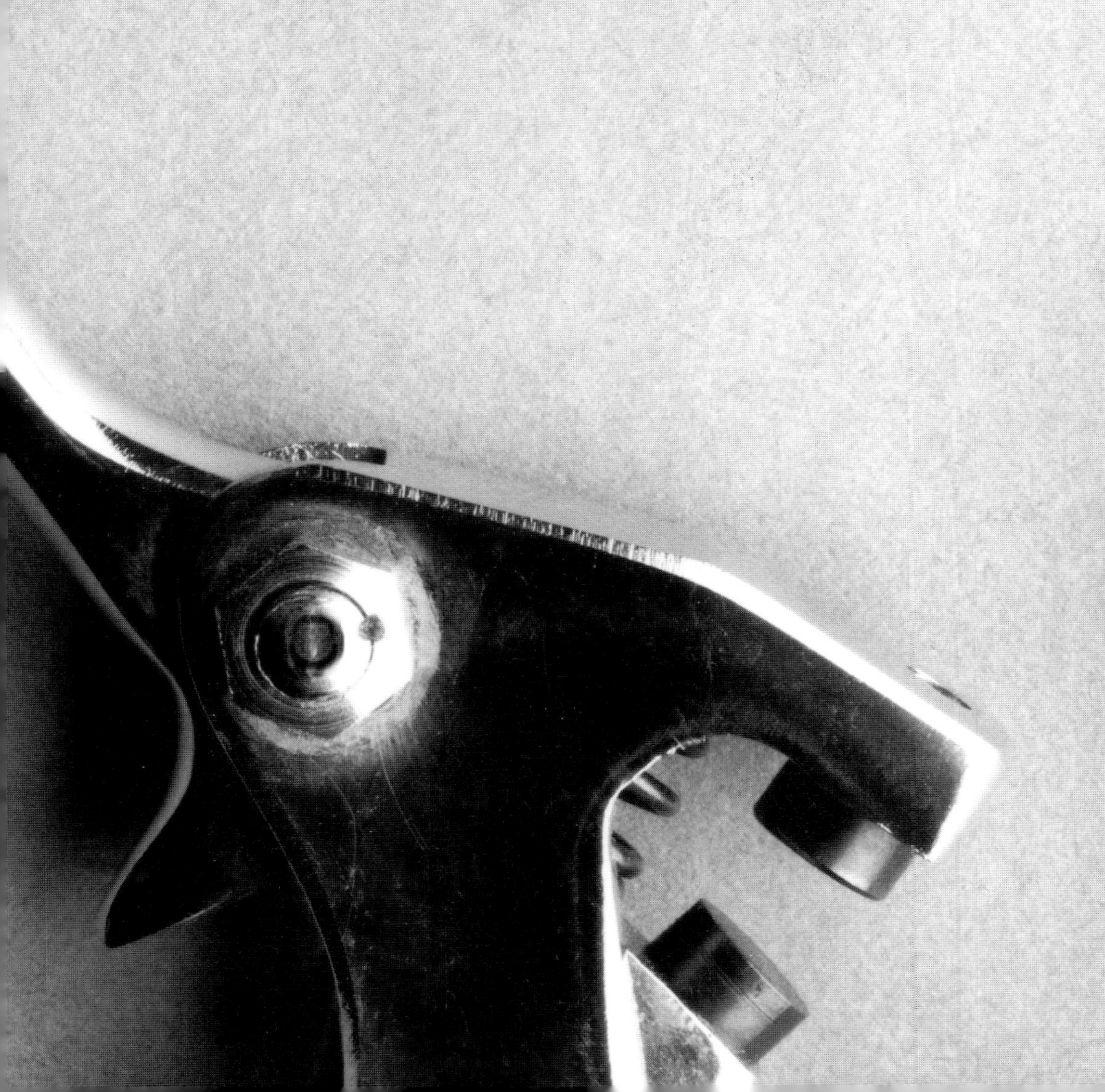

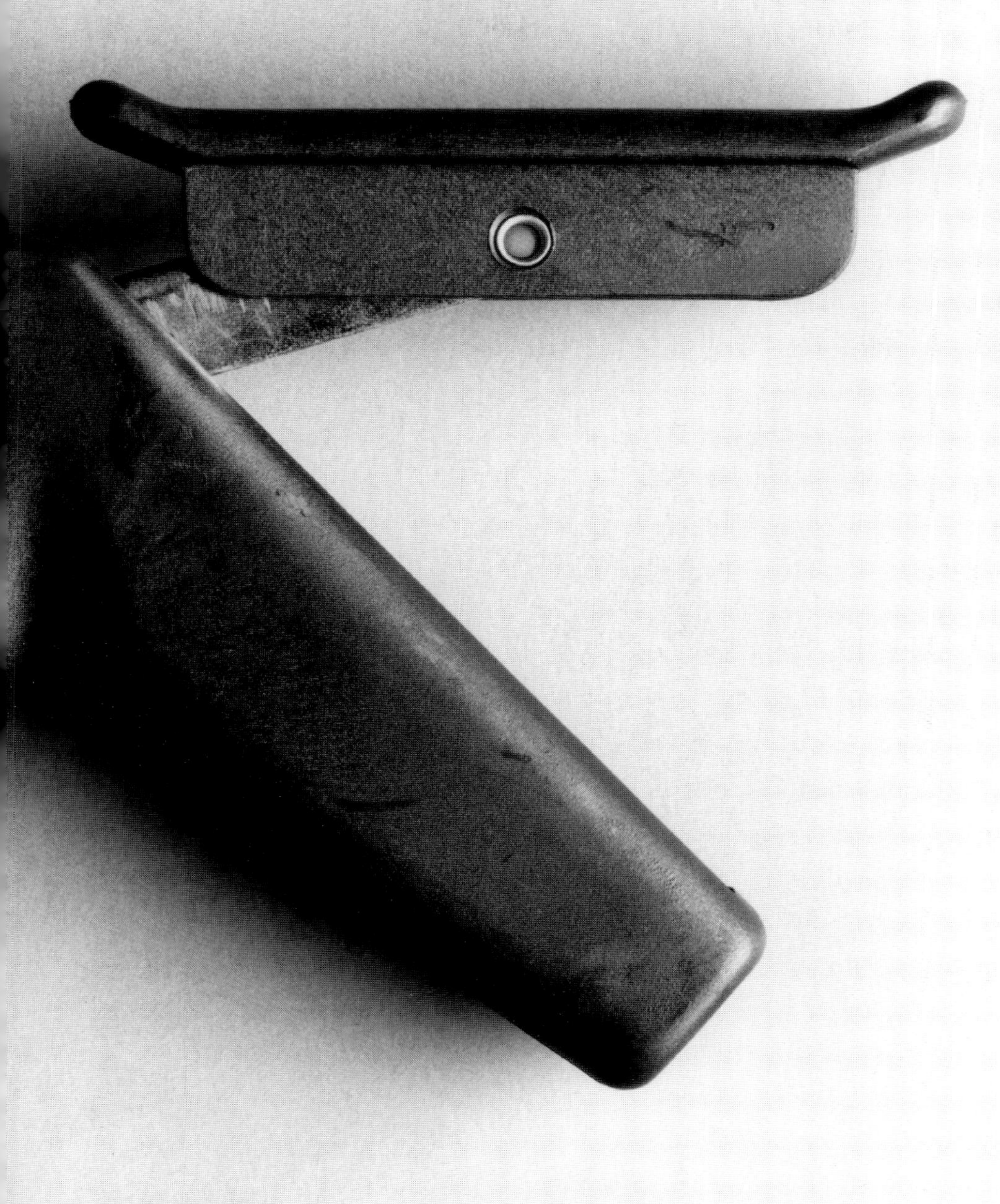

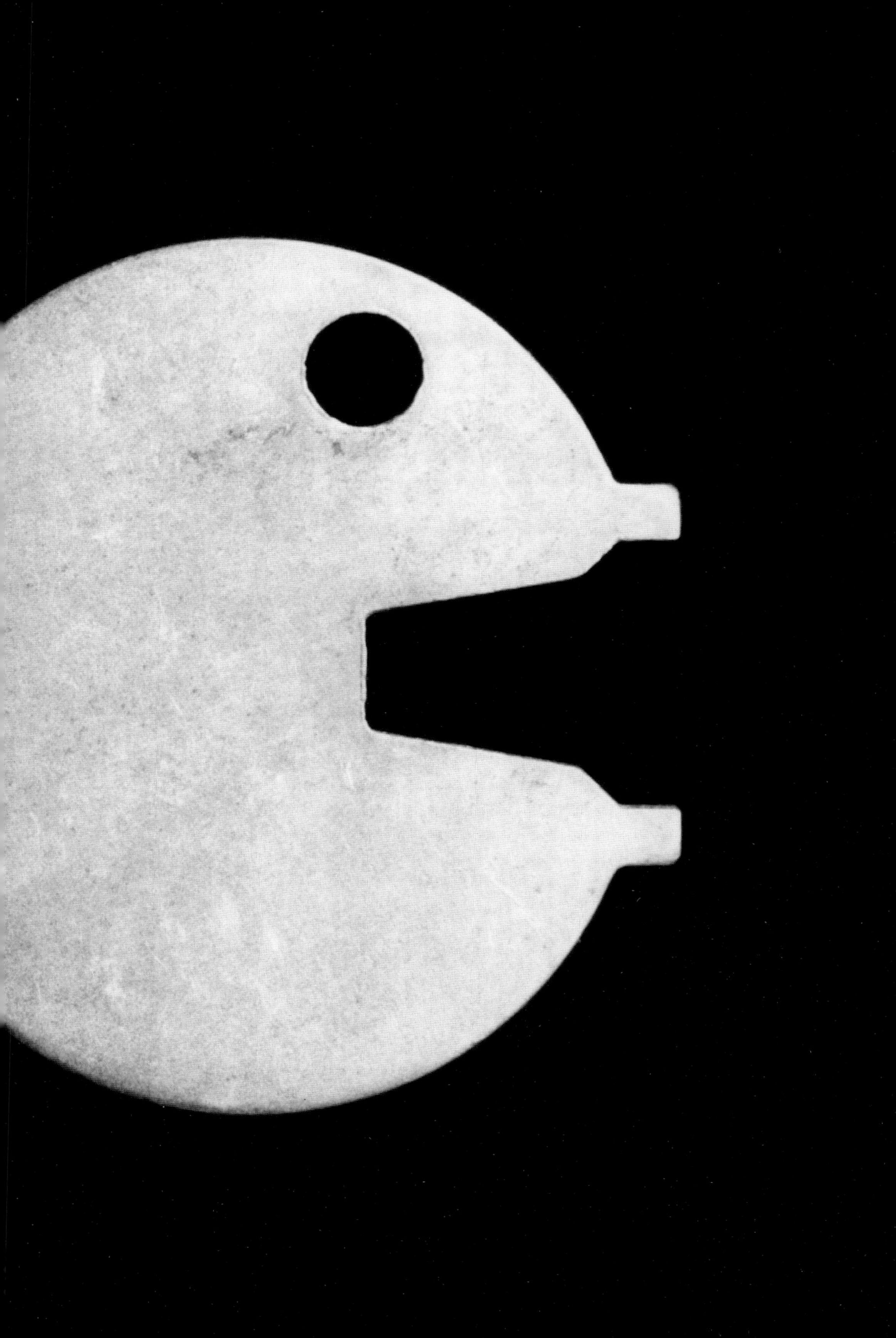

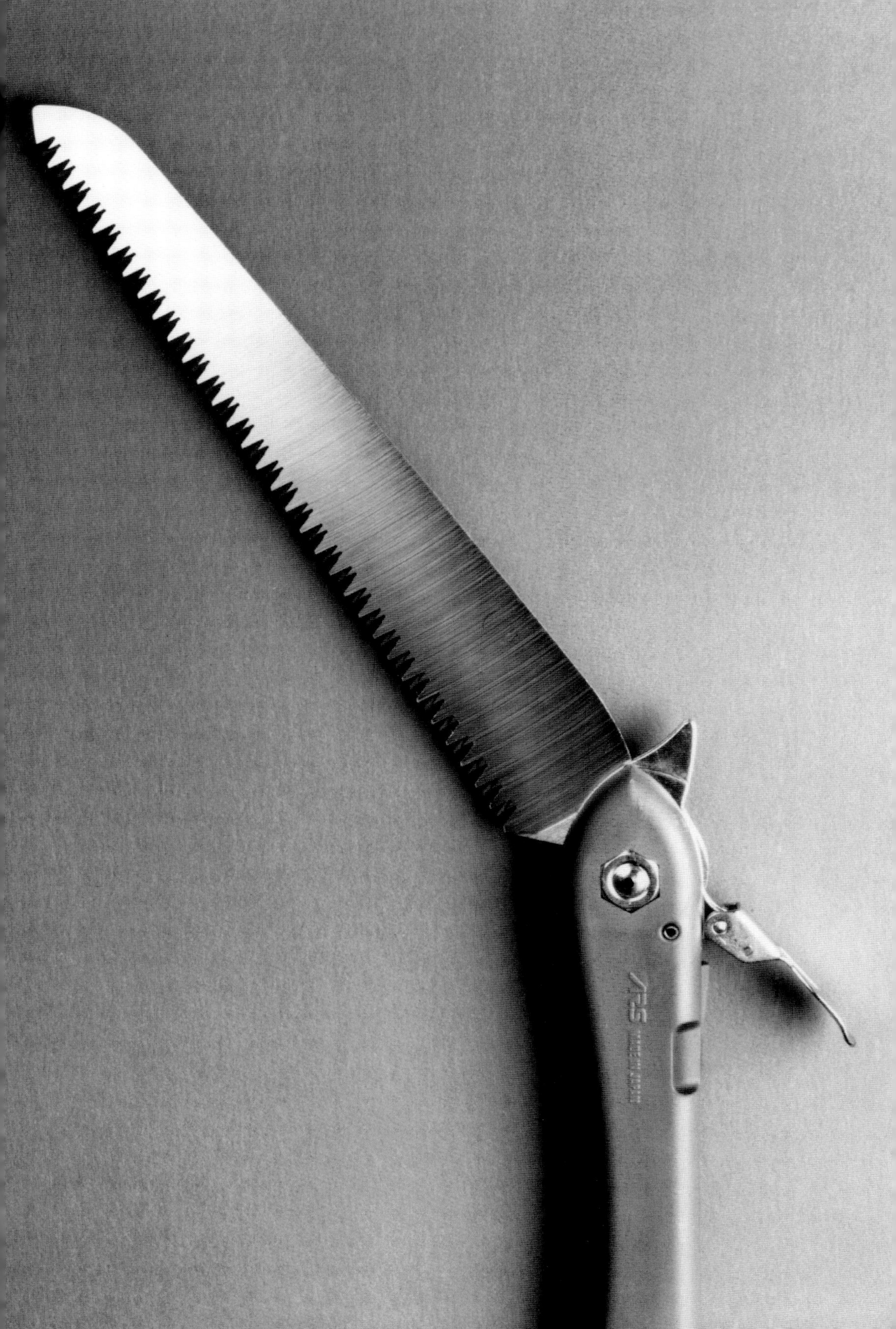

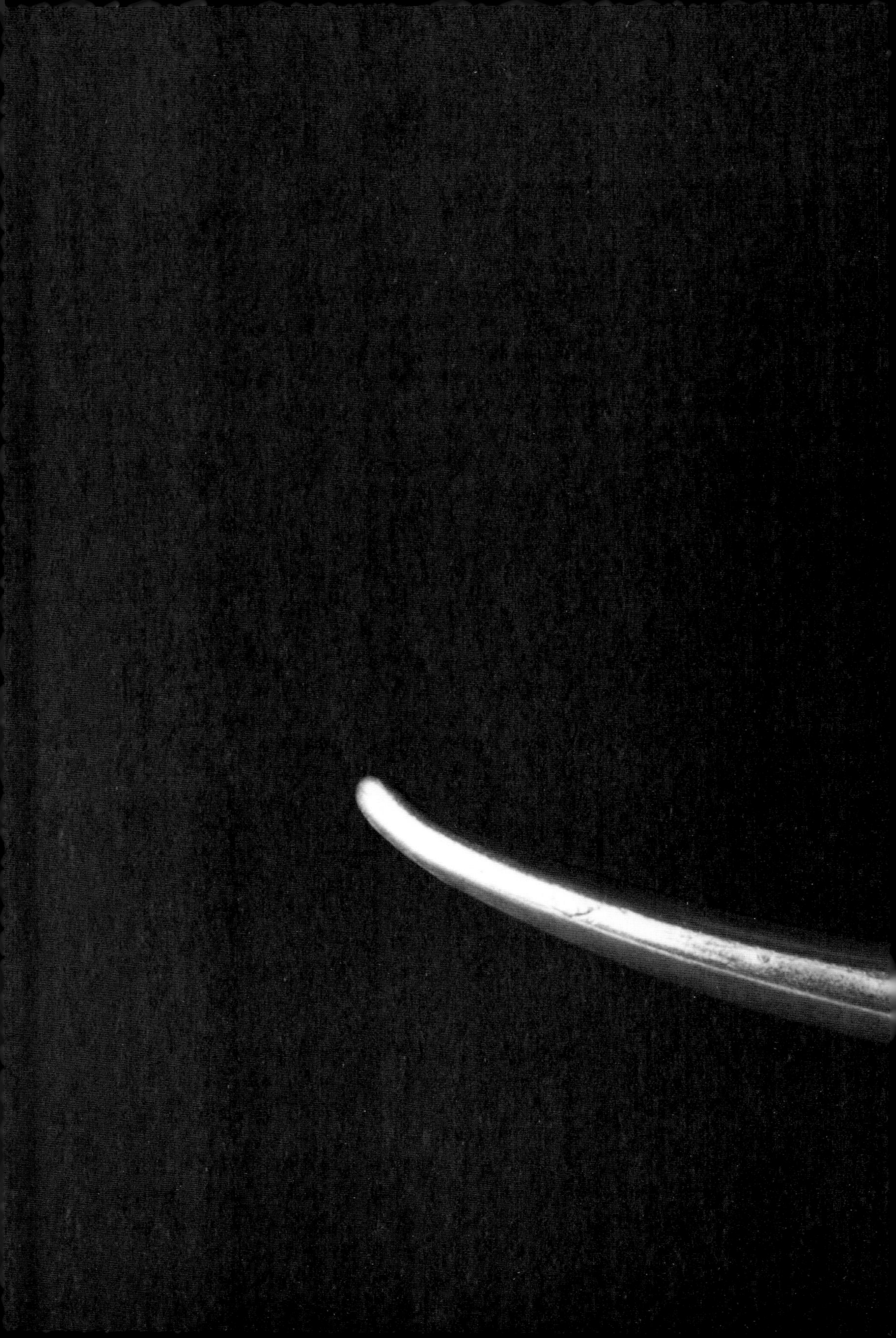

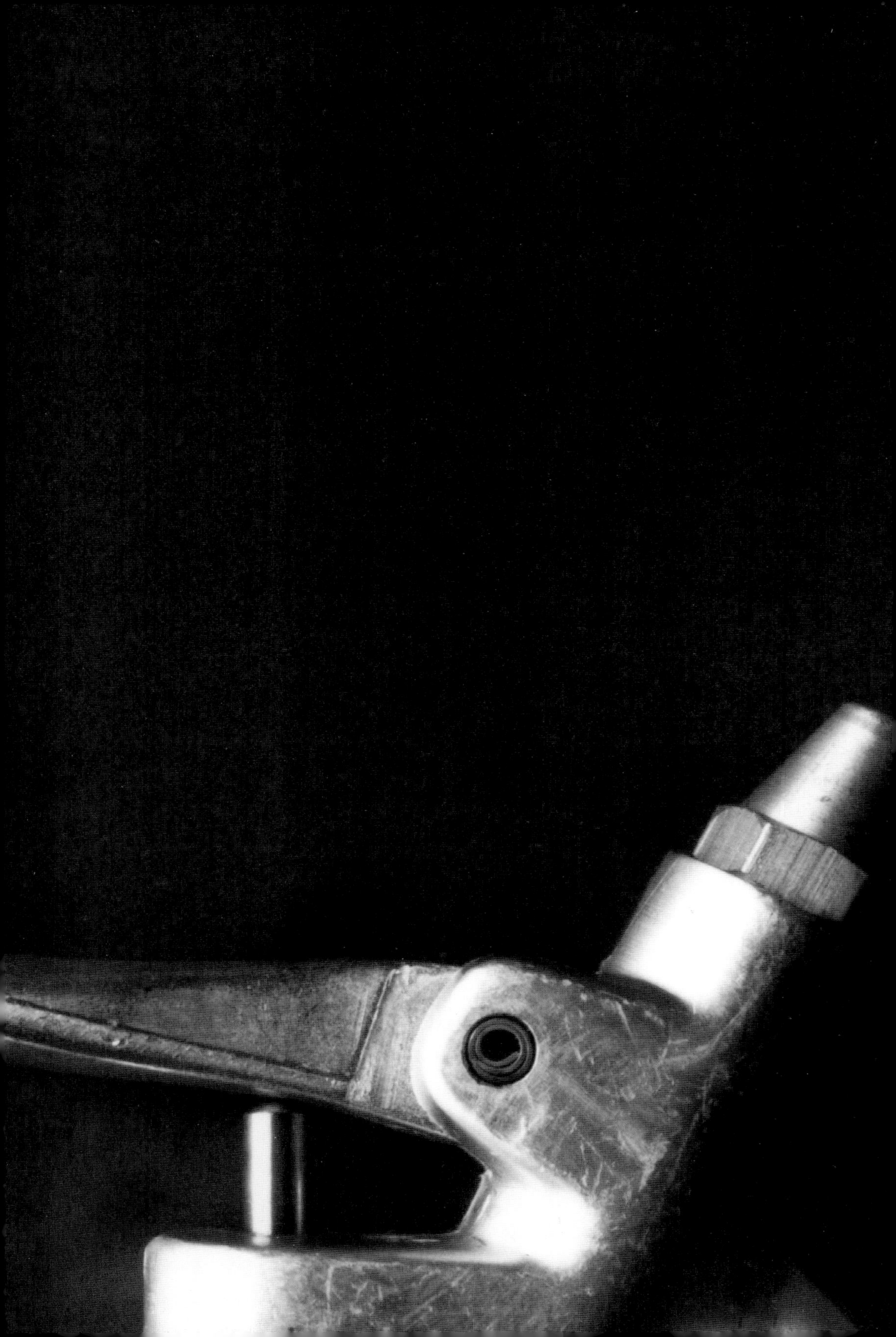

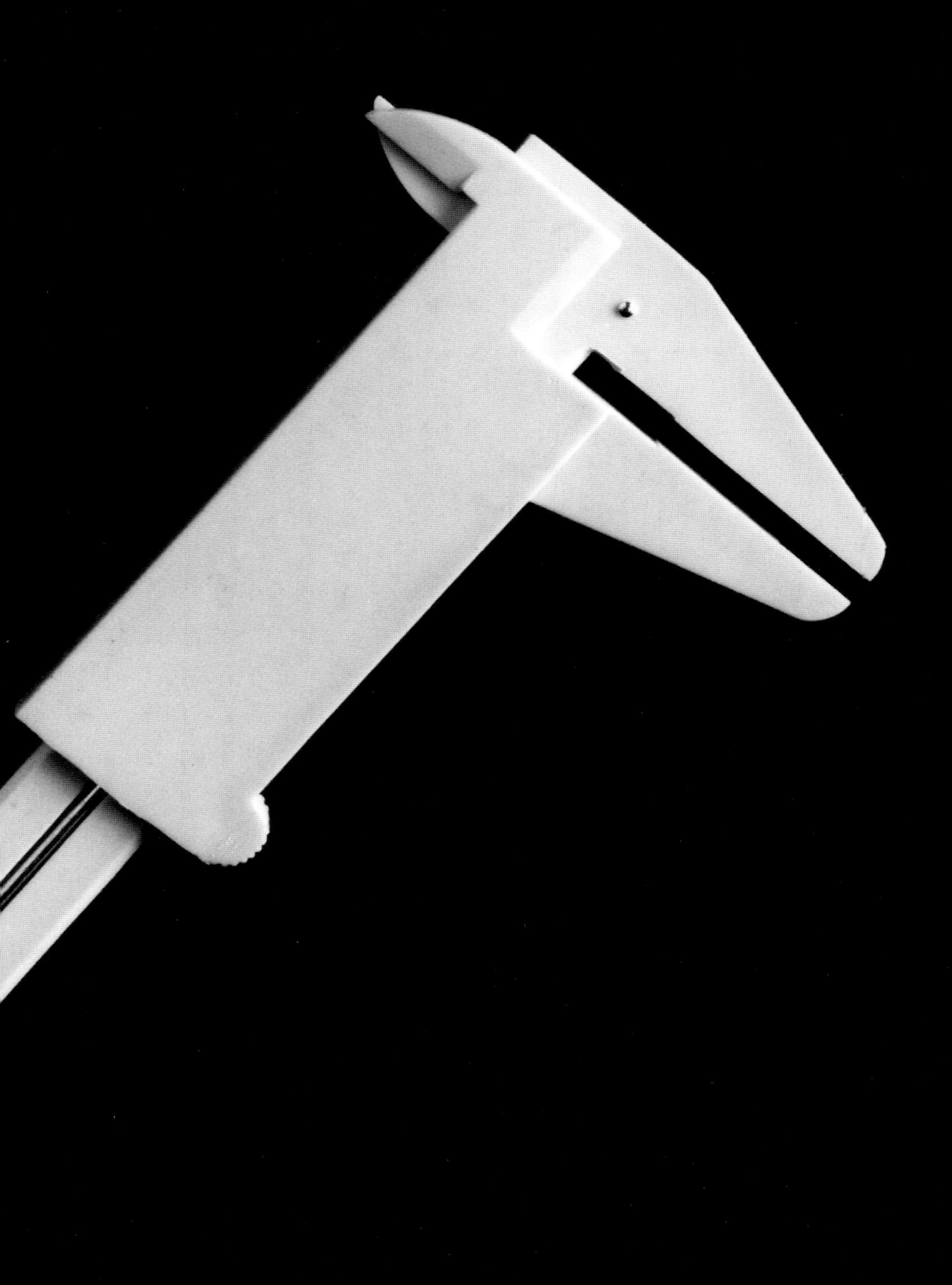

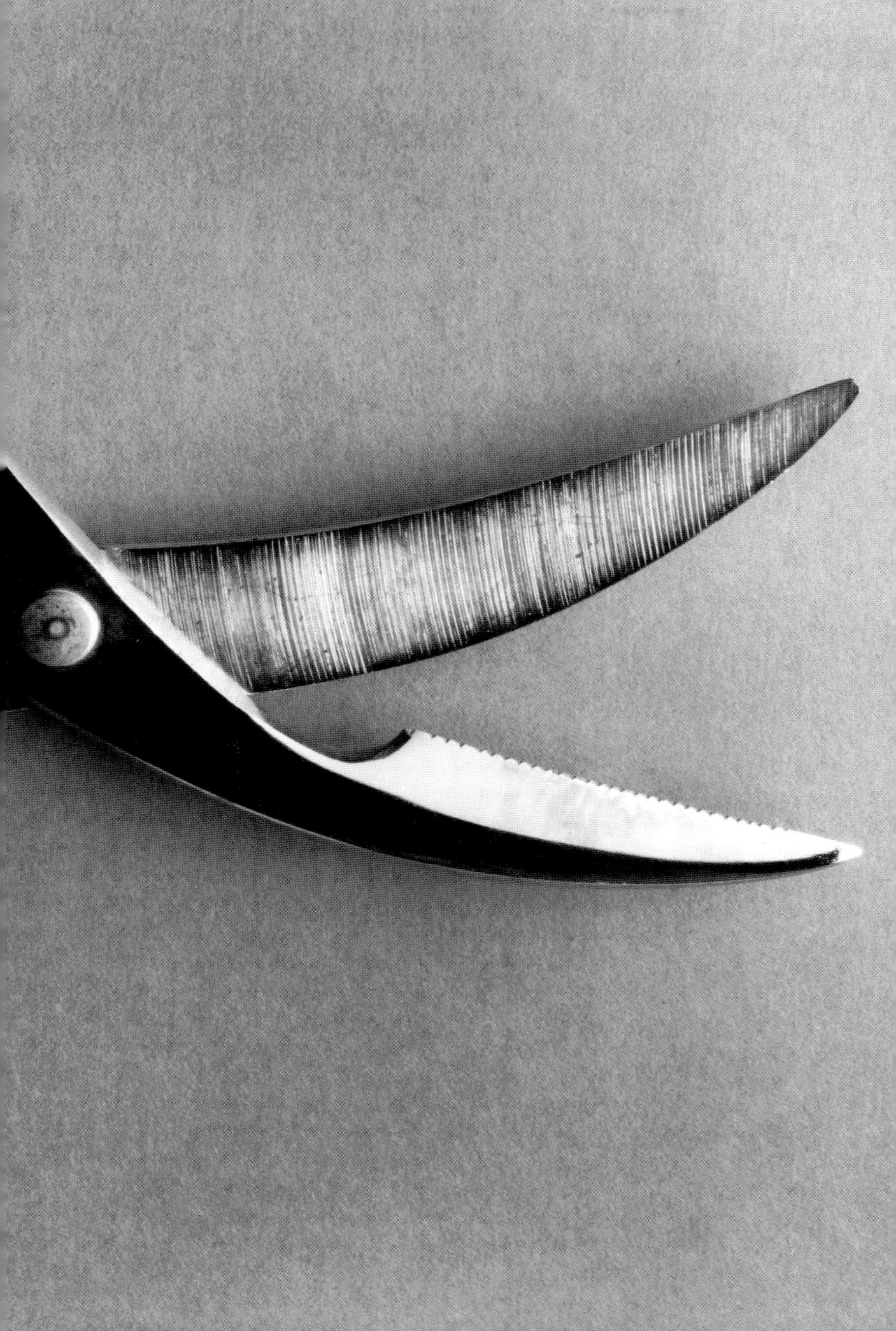

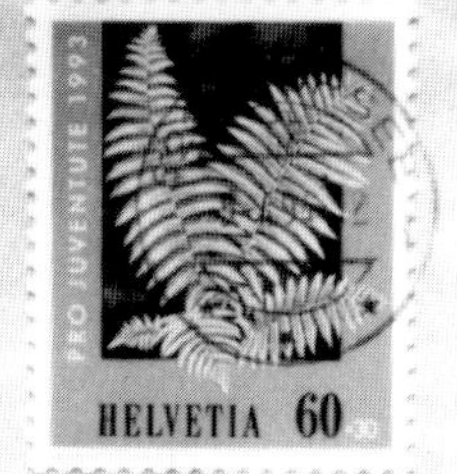

ALEX ROBERT
FLUGZEUG- &
SCHIFFSKONSTRUKTEUR
FREIESTRASSE 119
8032 ZUERICH

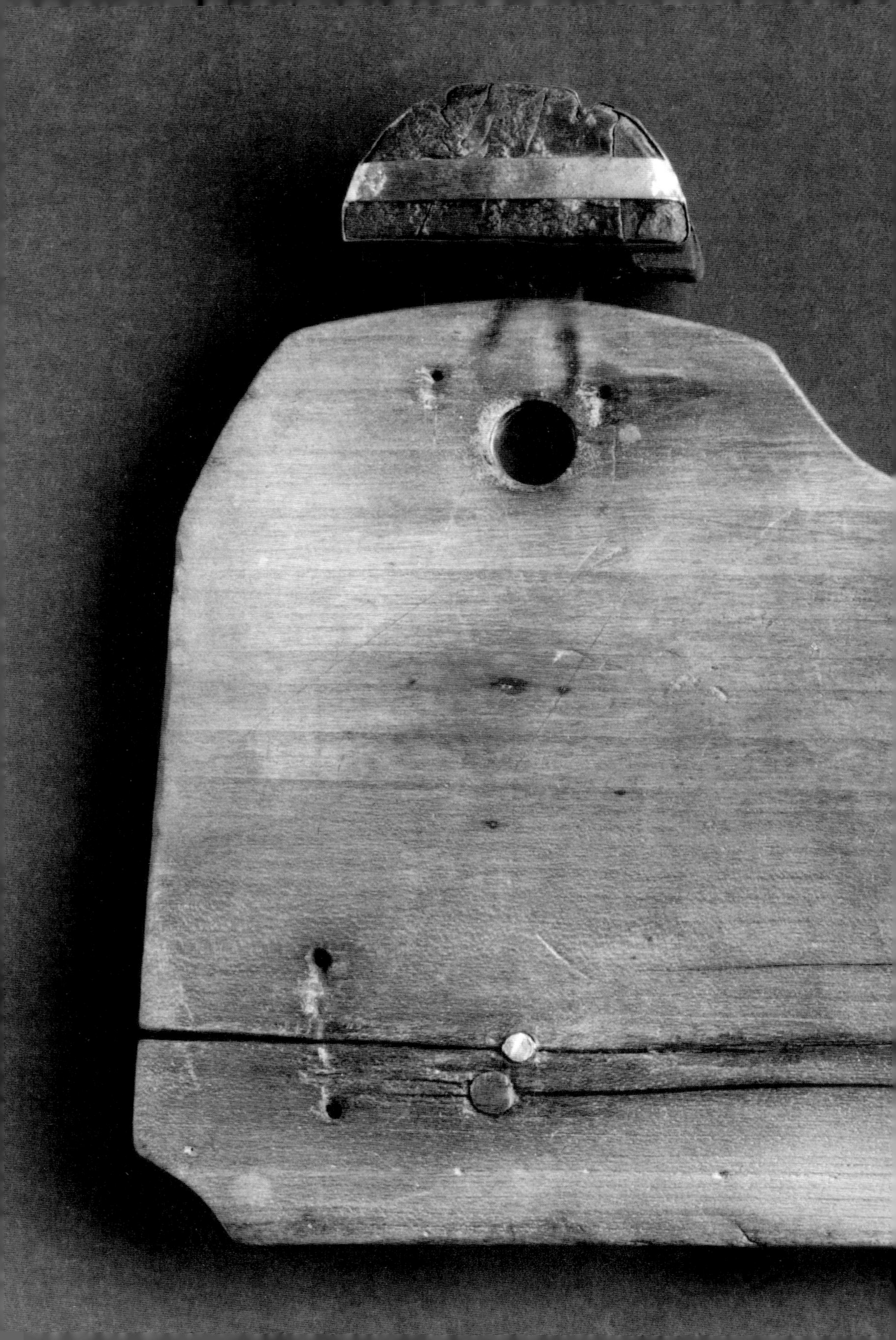

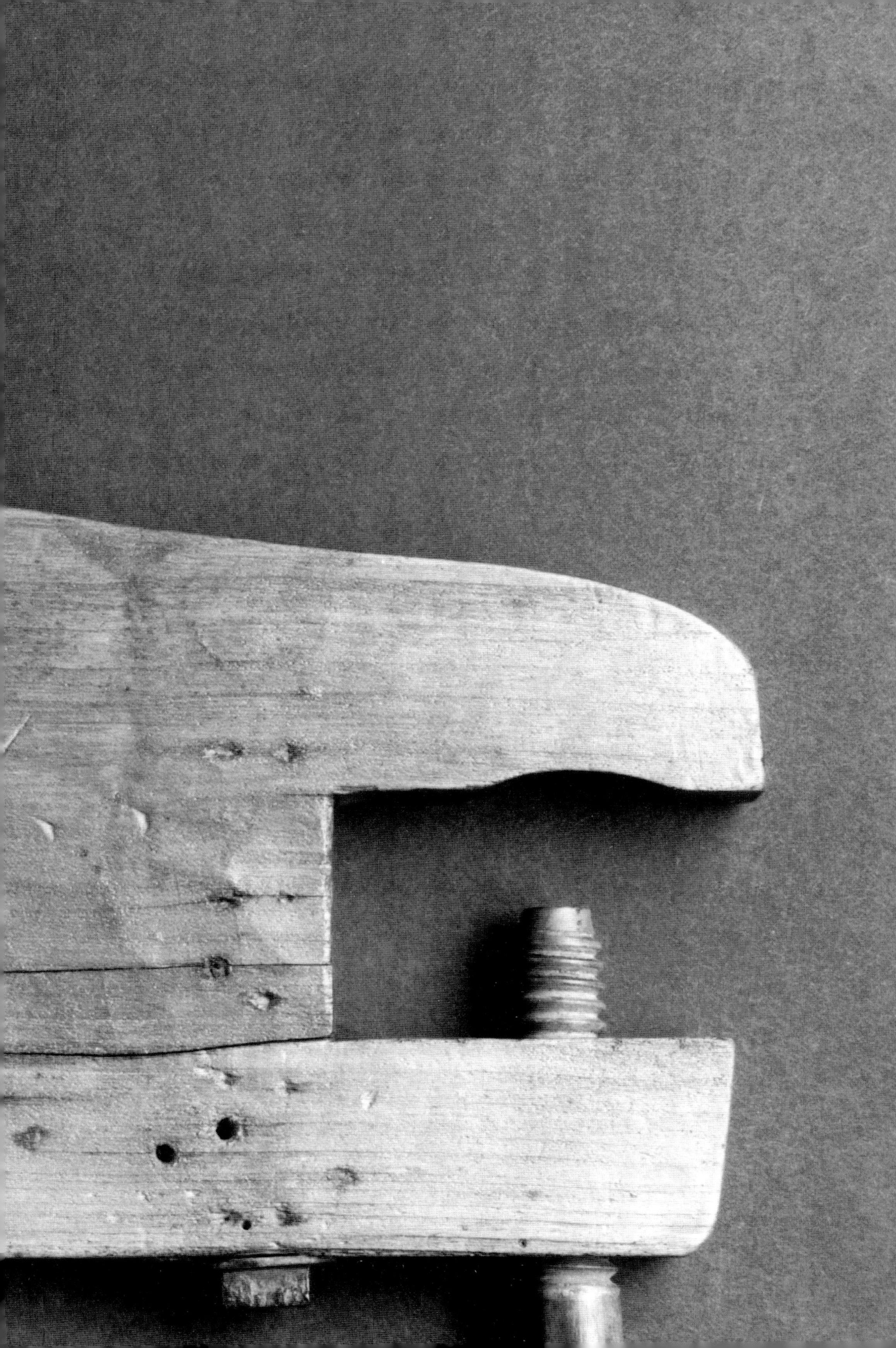

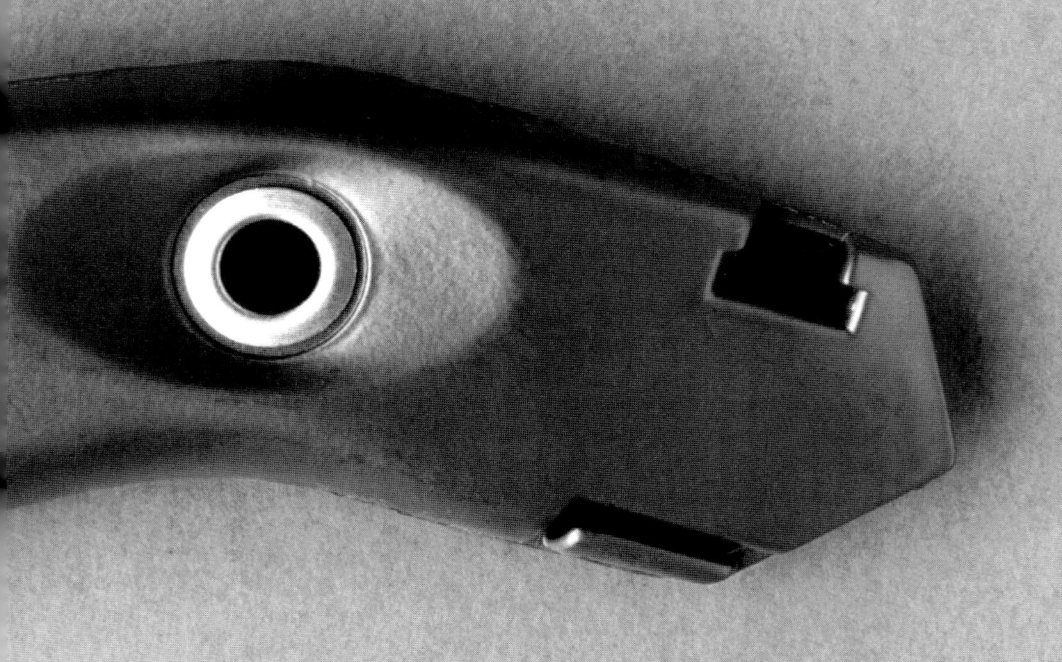

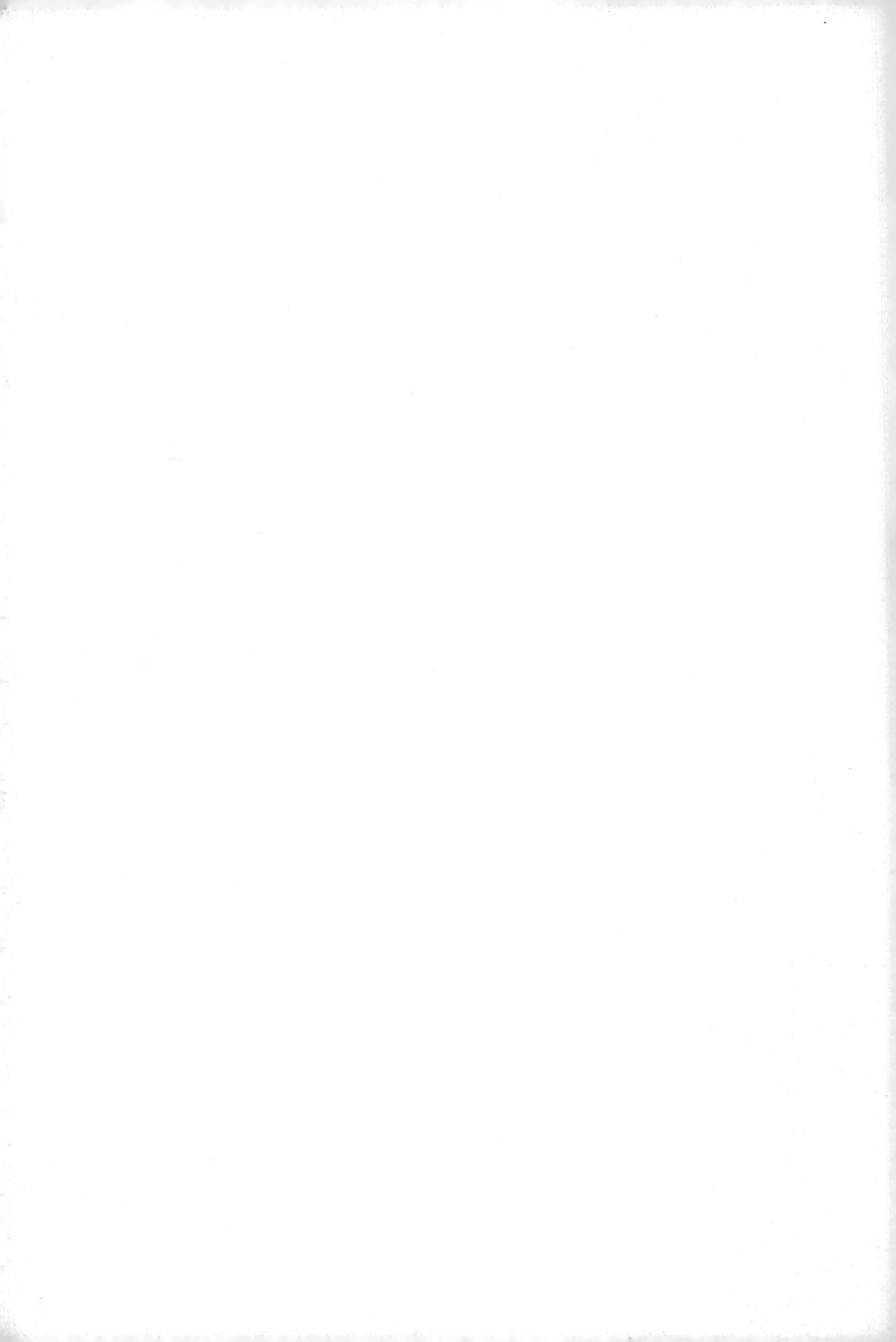

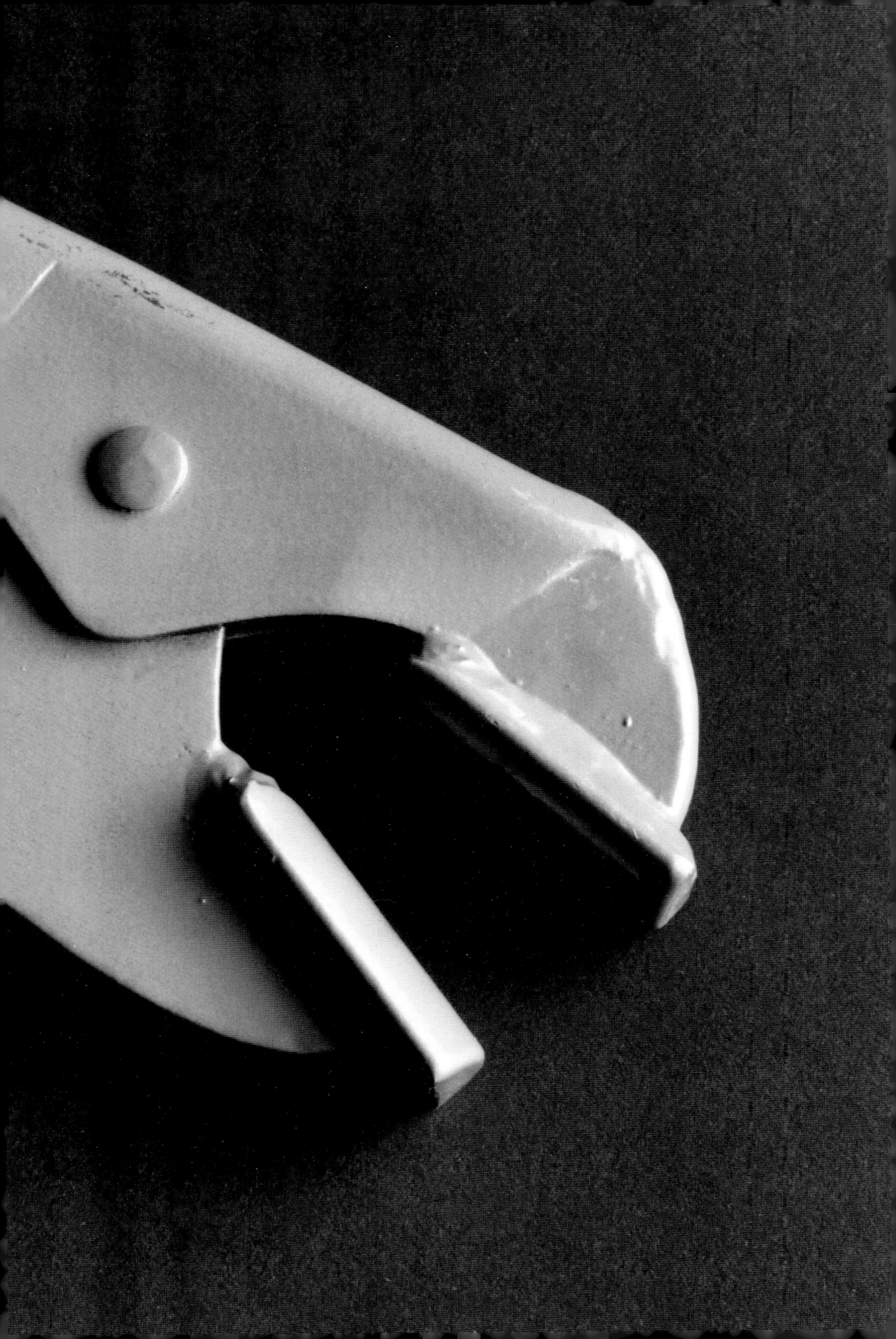

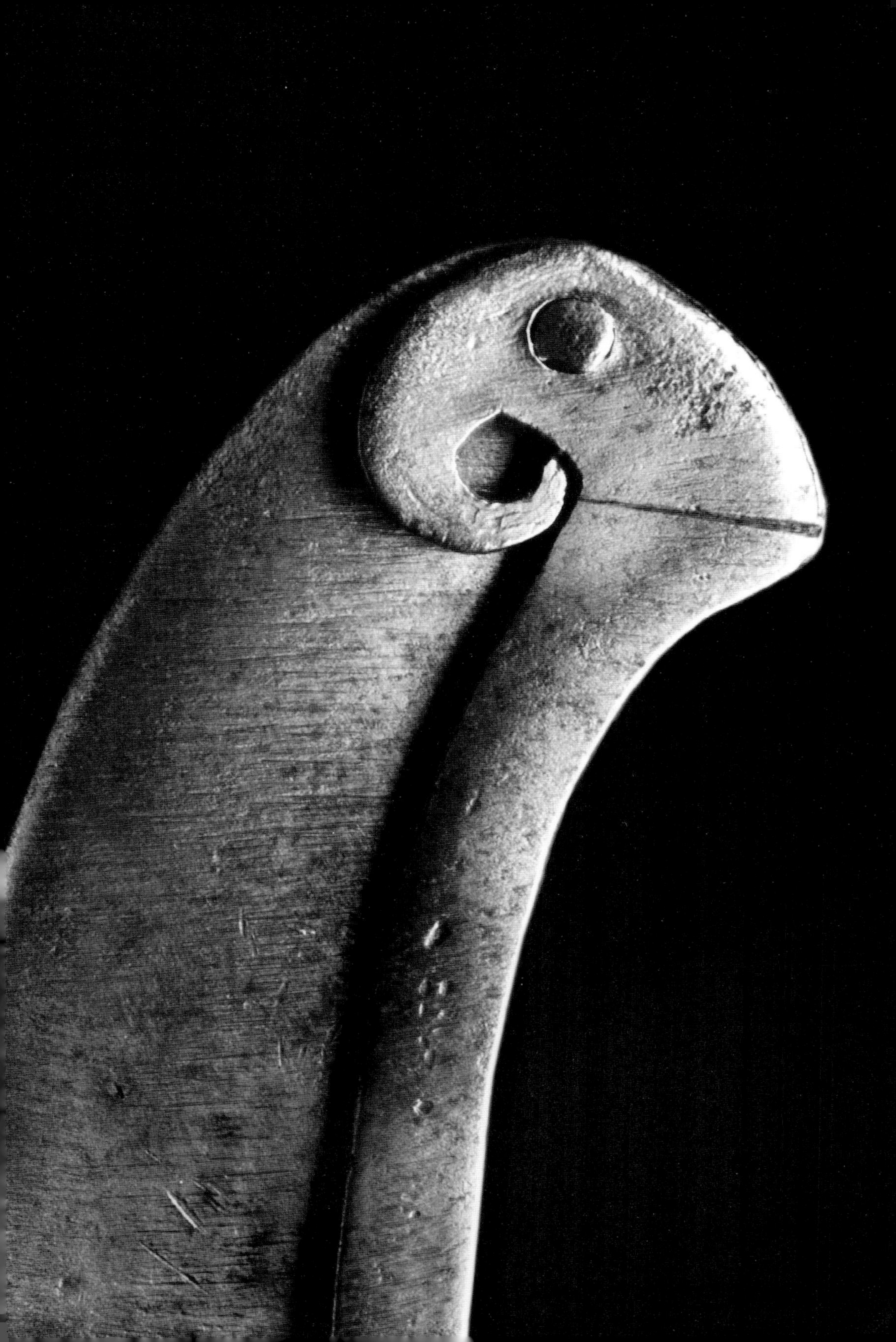

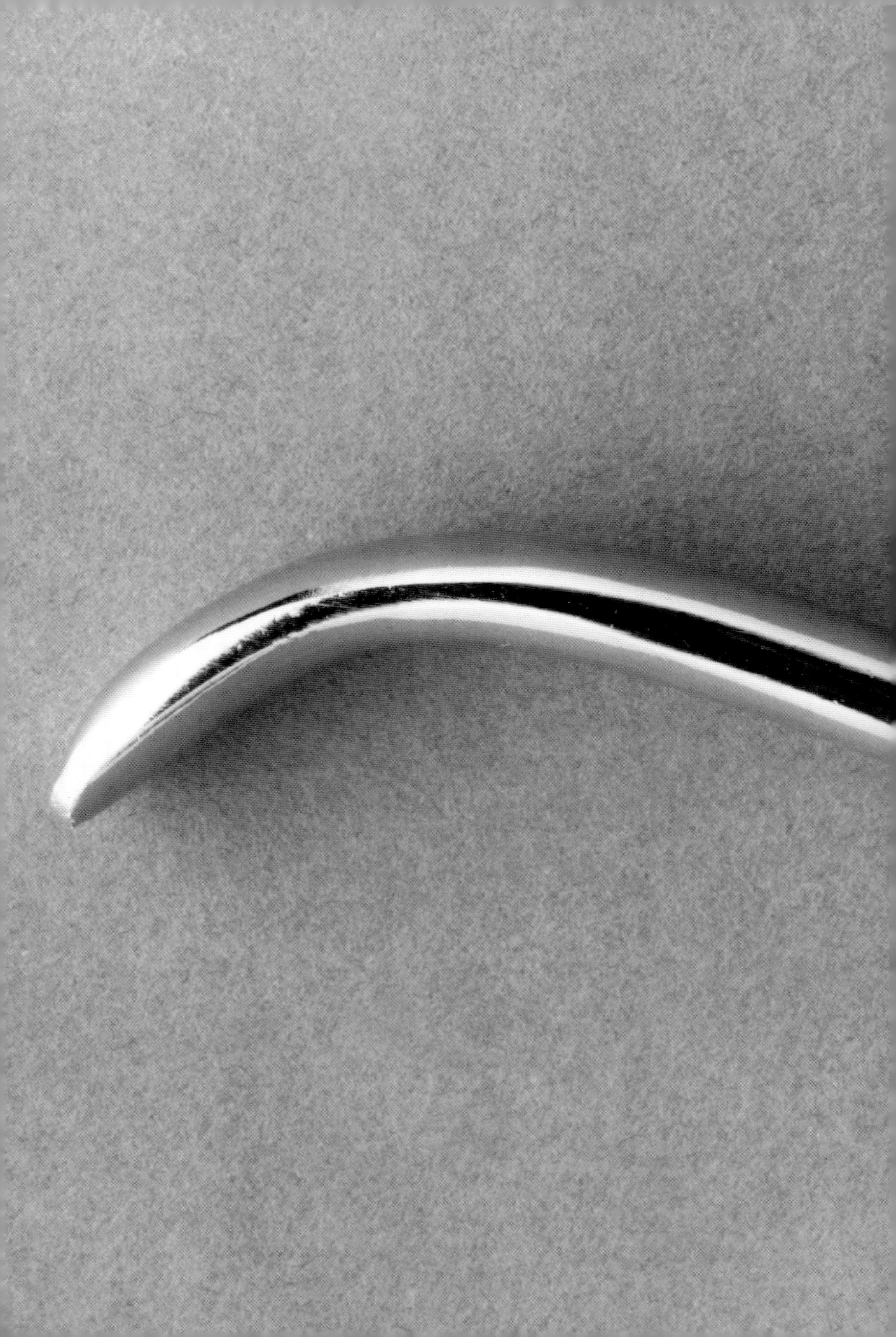

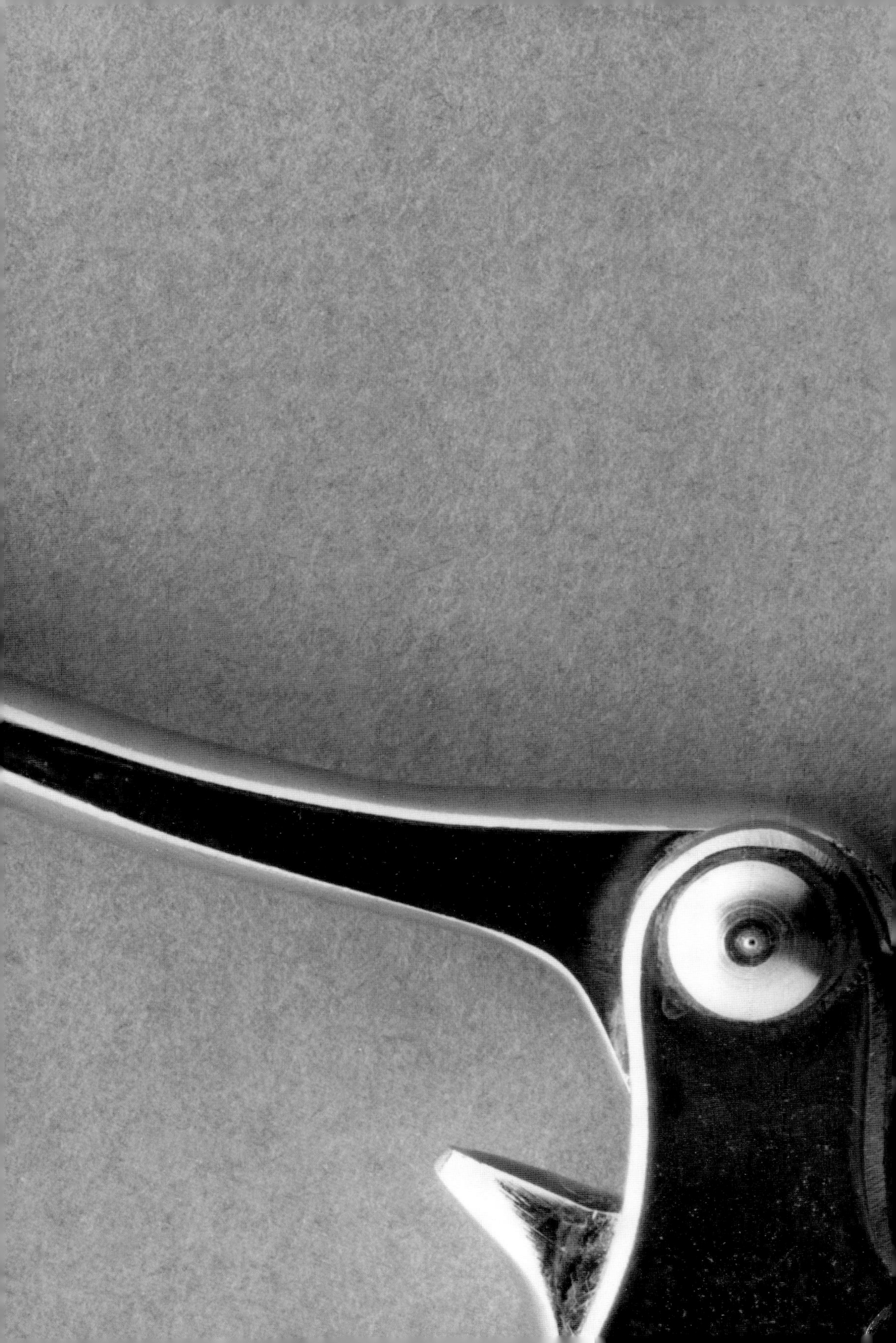

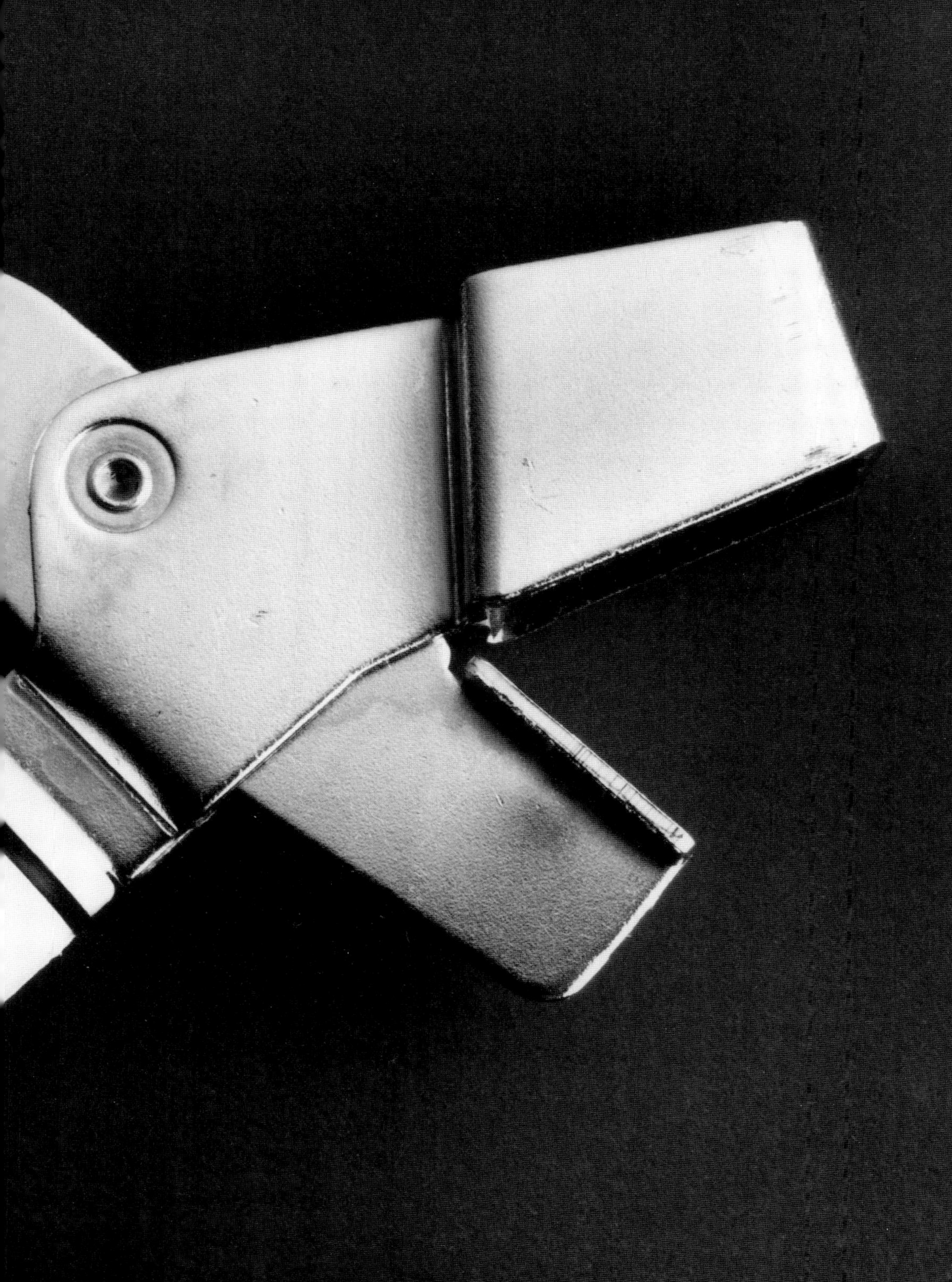

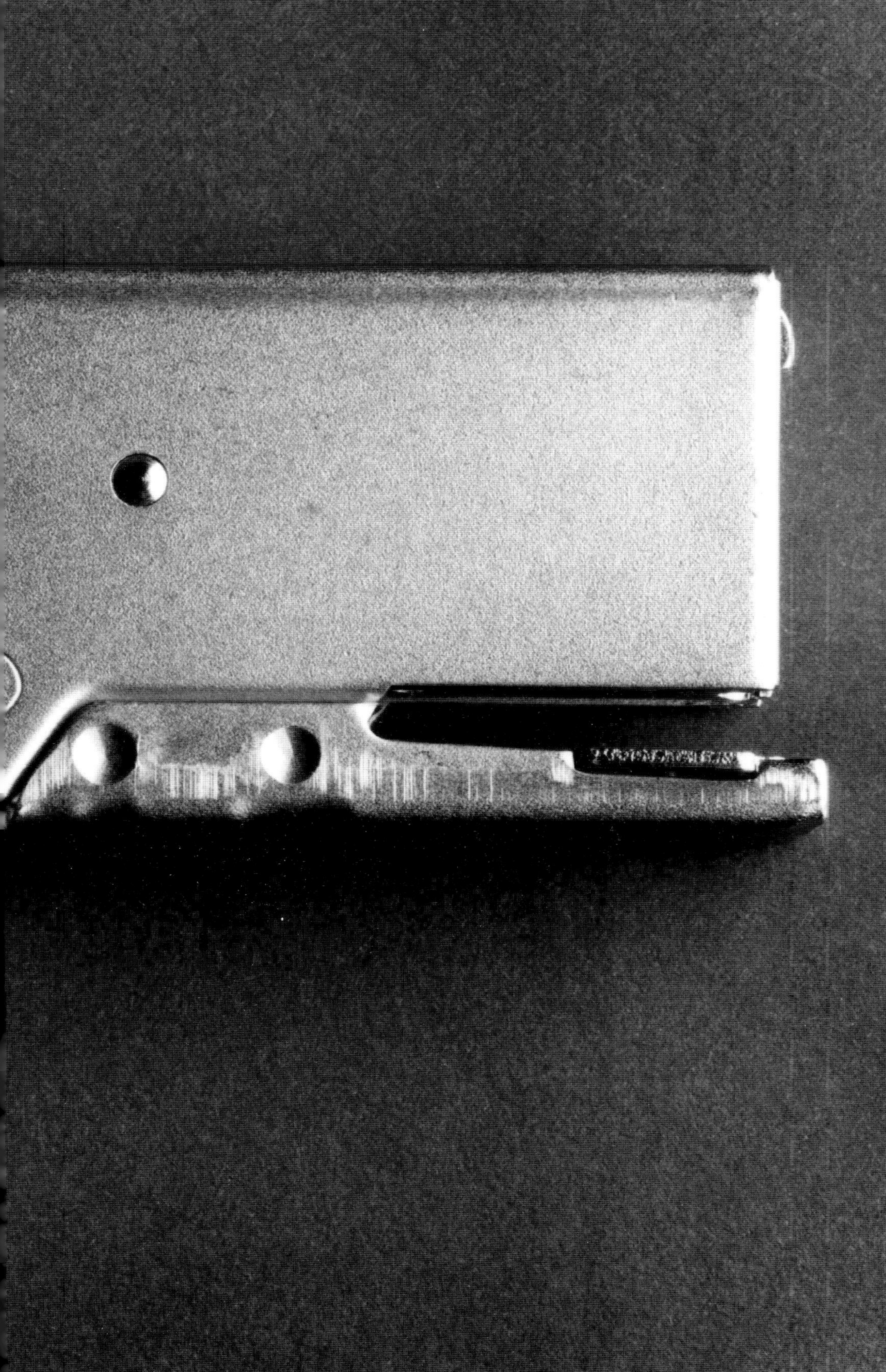

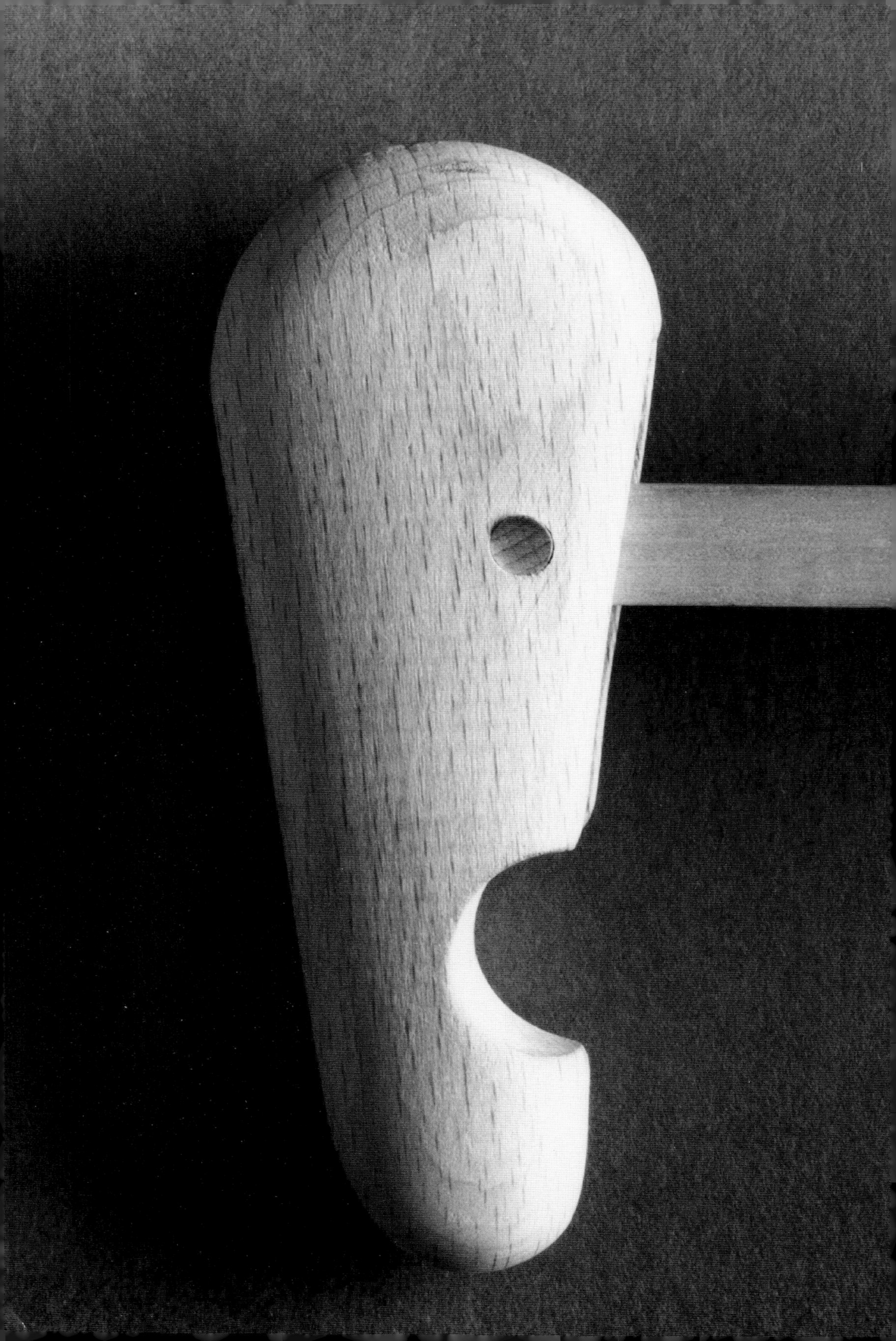

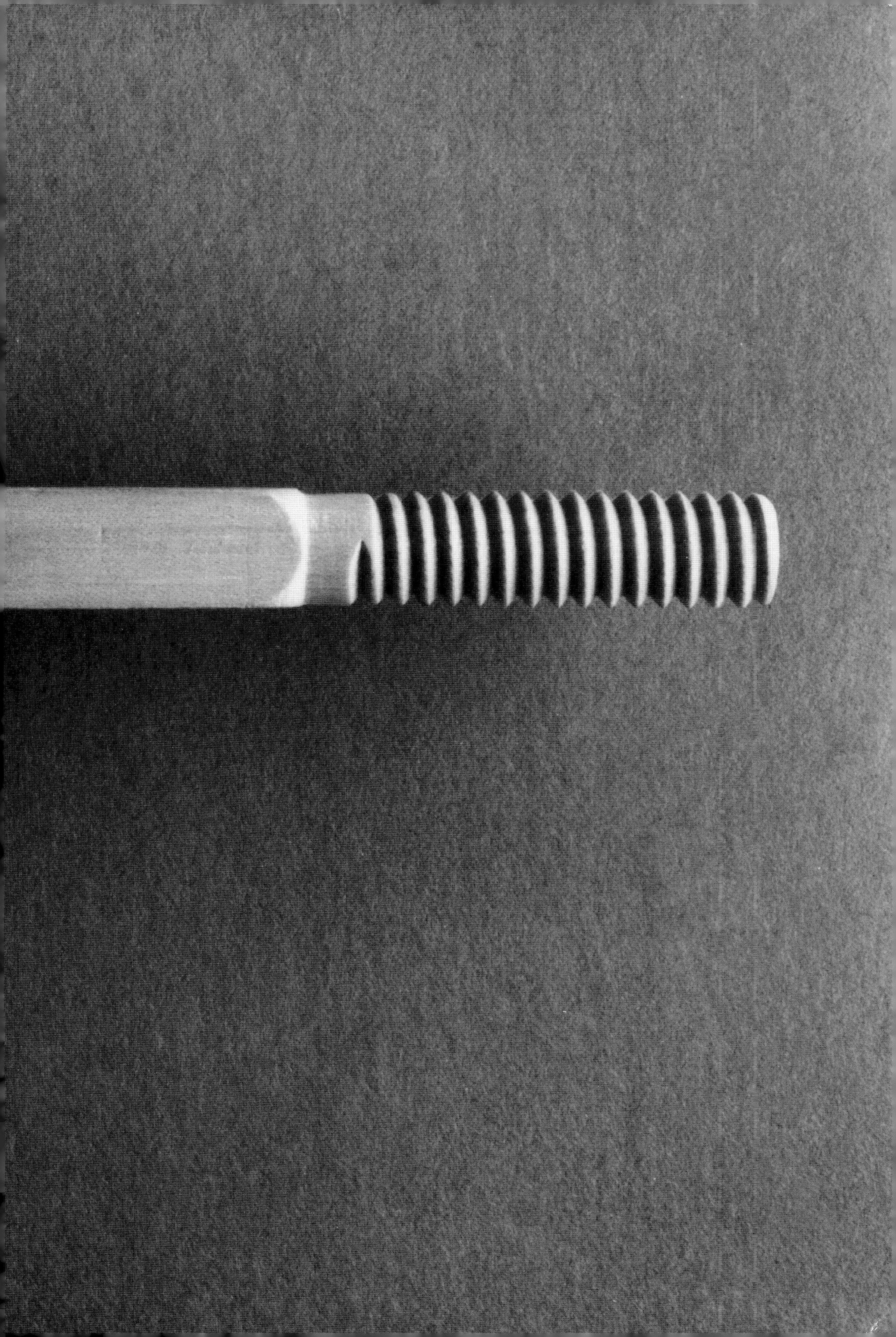

Years ago, we saw a padlock gazing at us with whimsical intensity. It occurred to us that seeing is selection, a process of framing. When it comes to photography you might call it mental cropping. As we began consciously selecting and framing and cropping, the world became a delightfully communicative universe of human and animal faces – eyes, noses, and mouths – that tell a never-ending stream of silent stories. These adventures in vision are only the tip of the iceberg, the first step in exploring the potential of projected realities. Now choose your mood, take a look around you, wherever you are, and watch for faces that will haunt and hearten you.

François and Jean Robert

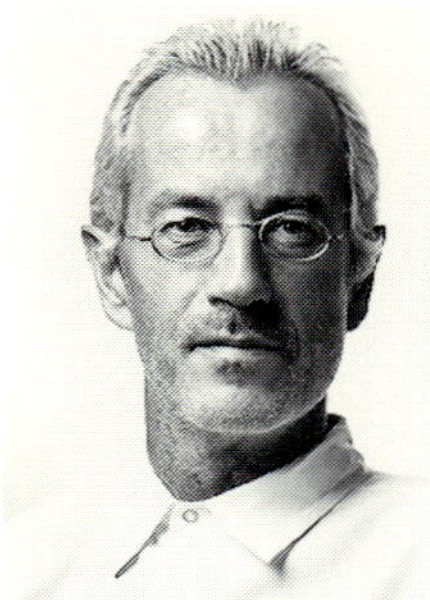

François Robert

1946	Born in La Chaux-de-Fonds, Switzerland
1968	Graduates from L'Ecole des Beaux Arts, Lausanne
1968–71	Graphic designer for Pirelli Industries, Milan
1971–72	Graphic designer for Unimark International, Johannesburg
1972–73	Graphic designer for Unimark International, Chicago
1973–79	Graphic design studio in Chicago
1979	Photographic studio in Chicago

Publications

Graphis, 1979

Before and After, 1981

A Day in the Life of America, 1985

Communication Arts, 1988

The Color of Fashion, 1988

One-person shows

Nikon Gallery, Zurich

Betsy Rosenfield Gallery, Chicago

The Chicago Cultural Center and

the Field Museum, Chicago

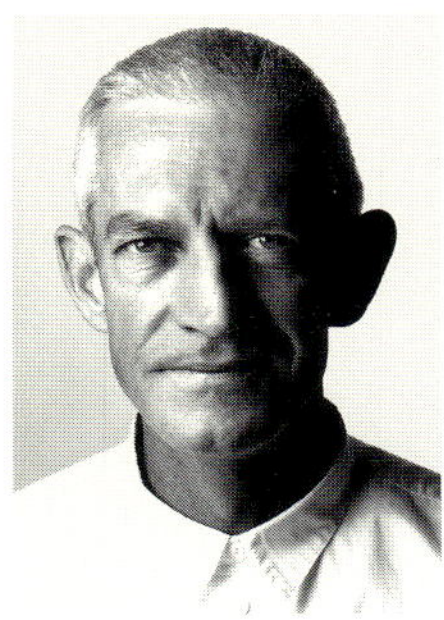

Jean Robert

1945	Born in La Chaux-de-Fonds, Switzerland
1968	Graduates from L'Ecole des Arts et Métiers, La Chaux-de-Fonds
1969–71	Graphic designer for Pirelli Industries, Milan
1971–72	Graphic designer for Unimark International, London
1972	Senior graphic designer at Pentagram Design, London
1977	Returns to Switzerland and opens his own graphic design studio with his partner Käti Durrer in Zurich

Member of

Alliance Graphic International, AGI

Art Director's Club Switzerland, ADC

Teaching activities

1981, 83	Guest lecturer, Ohio State University, Columbus
1984–86	Graphic Design Department, School of Design, Zurich
1990	Guest lecturer, School of Graphic Design, Lucerne

Thanks

Rudolf Barmettler, John Boehm, Harri Boller, Tom Carlson, John Mc Connell, Alan Fletcher, Bob Feie, Colin Forbes, Jane Gittings, Ron Gordon, Richard Gorman, Alfredo W. Häberli, Franziska and Bruno Mancia-Bodmer, Lars Müller, Alex Robert, Käti Robert-Durrer, Catherine Schelbert, Heidy Schuppisser, Stuart Schwartz, Barry Weaver

Design: Robert & Durrer, Zurich

Lithos & DTP: Mancia-Bodmer, FBM Studio, Zurich

Printing: Waser Druck AG, Buchs/ZH

Binding: Buchbinderei Burkhardt AG, Mönchaltorf/ZH

ISBN 3-906700-99-2 Hardcover

ISBN 3-907044-17-7 Softcover

Lars Müller Publishers, 5401 Baden/Switzerland

Printed in Switzerland